American Business Abroad

Six Lectures on Direct Investment

American Business Abroad

Six Lectures on Direct Investment

by Charles P. Kindleberger

New Haven and London, Yale University Press, 1969

Library of Congress catalog card number: 69–12325
ISBN: 0–300–01096–6 (cloth), 0–300–01085–0 (paper)

Designed by Marvin Howard Simmons,
set in Baskerville type,
and printed in the United States of America by
The Colonial Press, Inc., Clinton, Massachusetts.

Published in Great Britain, Europe, and Africa by
Yale University Press, Ltd., London.
Distributed in Canada by McGill-Queen's University
Press, Montreal; in Latin America by Kaiman & Polon,
Inc., New York City; in Australasia and Southeast
Asia by John Wiley & Sons Australasia Pty. Ltd.,
Sydney; in India by UBS Publishers' Distributors Pvt.,
Ltd., Delhi; in Japan by John Weatherhill, Inc., Tokyo.

Preface

In the summer of 1966 I had the honor of serving as Visiting Erskine Fellow at the University of Canterbury in Christchurch, New Zealand. In preparing for the visit I outlined a series of lectures on direct investment against the possibility that I would be called upon for a connected discourse. As it happened there was greater interest in a variety of topics, so that there was no occasion to present the lectures. There was, however, an opportunity to start writing them. Three and a half were finished by the time I returned. Other commitments and pressures diverted my attention from the subject, and the project languished.

In the academic year of 1967–68, on leave from the Massachusetts Institute of Technology and teaching at the Atlanta University Center, I brought along a substantial volume of books on European economic history, which I proposed to teach at Morehouse College. The demand for the subject was exiguous, and the course was bracketed, or scrubbed. In the spring of 1968, however, I gave a seminar in international business at Atlanta University, and was asked by the Sloan School of Management at M.I.T. to prepare a course on the same subject in the fall of 1968. My small library on the subject was sent for. Old drafts were dusted off. Lectures five and six were written and the lot rewritten. Hence this short and compact book on direct investment which raises the larger questions of its role in the national and the international economy.

This is economics, not business administration. There is nothing on problems within the firm, which have received much attention and deserve more. There is no escape from legal problems, which are not treated but are flagged when we encounter them, or from the politics of the subject. One scholar asserts that it is impossible to separate economic and social goals, by which is presumably meant that it is impossible to separate the economics of direct investment from the politics. Perhaps so. But these disquisitions focus on the economics and only note when political issues of power, prestige, independence, neocolonial status, domination, and the like are brought into the debate. There is a trade-off, presumably, between political independence, prestige, or power, whether plus or minus, and economic goals such as income. Admittedly there are times when the two are positively correlated—complements, instead of substitutes. But the cobbler must stick to his last. This book is by an economist, and is heavily weighted on the economics of the question.

I have borrowed copiously from a paper on "Public Policy and the International Corporation," submitted to the Subcommittee on Antitrust and Monopoly of the Senate Committee on the Judiciary in April 1966, and published in *International Aspects of Antitrust, Hearings* Before the Subcommittee on Antitrust and Monopoly of the Committee on the Judiciary, United States Senate, 89th Congress, Second Session (Washington, D.C., G.P.O., 1967), Part 1, pp. 162–73. My thanks are due M. A. Adelman, Carl Beigie, Stephen H. Hymer, and Raymond Vernon, who furnished comments on that paper. Donald G. Heckerman, Klaus Stegemann, and again Professor Hymer were kind enough to comment on the first draft of the first four lectures. My thanks are also due seminar and lecture audiences in Dunedin, Canberra, Sydney, and Nashville for critical comment on some of the ideas to be set forth. A précis of these ideas, with even less political content, was presented in Chapter 21 of the 4th edition of *International Economics* (Homewood, Ill., Richard D. Irwin, 1968).

Above all, let me thank A. D. Brownlie and the Department of Economics of the University of Canterbury for their generous hospitality during five stimulating weeks in New Zealand.

C. P. K.

Atlanta, Georgia
April 1968

Contents

The Theory of Direct Investment

There is no single obvious principle for organizing a topic as complex as direct investment—sometimes also referred to as the international corporation or the multi-national corporation. One organizational choice lies between theoretical analysis and empirical description; another, within description, between classification by industry—between, say, manufacturing and mining plus extraction—and by geographical area or level of development. In what follows we compromise. The first and last lectures are devoted to theory, the theory of direct investment and of the international corporation, respectively. Sandwiched between them are four treatments with an ostensibly geographic orientation. The second lecture is on the interests of the United States, which have been the source of many or most of the newcomer firms to the ranks of direct investors or international corporations, and enjoys or suffers the problems of the situs of the parent companies. Three subsequent lectures are focused primarily by regions—although many of the problems treated in each are general to all—Europe and Japan, the Dominions, and the less developed countries.

Direct Investment as a Capital Movement

Direct investment used to be thought of by economists as an international capital movement. Capital movements take place in a variety of forms—through the issue of new securities, largely bonds; through purchases and sales of outstanding securities, both stocks and bonds, on security exchanges; through a variety of short-term credit instruments and forms; and through direct investment. Direct investment differed from other kinds of international capital movements in that it was accompanied by varying degrees of control, plus technology and management. But it was a capital movement.

For some purposes, and especially in the concerns of the United States, the capital movement features of direct investment remain paramount. Plagued by a balance-of-payments deficit, the United States imposed a set of voluntary controls on direct investment in February 1965 and converted them to mandatory restrictions in January 1968. More, much more, on this below. There is, in addition, renewed interest in the capital aspects of direct investment from a theoretical point of view, and particularly in the way national capital markets can be joined internationally through the markets for whole companies, in contrast with securities traded in organized markets. This subject will also occupy us later. But economists trying to interpret direct investment as a capital movement were struck by several peculiar phenomena. In the first place, investors often failed to take money with them when they went abroad to acquire control of a company; instead they would borrow in the local market. Capital movements would take place gross—the acquisition of an asset (an outflow) and the incurring of a liability (an inflow)—but not net. Or the investment would take place in kind, through the exchange of property—patents, technology, or machinery—against equity claims, without the normal transfer of funds through the foreign exchange associated with capital movements.

And direct investment would proceed by the reinvestment of profits, with the capital outflow matched by earnings on past investment, but again no movement of funds through the foreign-exchange market. On this showing the clue to direct investment lay in capital formation, not in capital movement.[1]

In the second place, direct investment often takes place simultaneously in two directions. United States companies invest in Europe, and European companies invest in the United States. Such two-way movements occur to some degree in securities, as investors seek to diversify their portfolios on the one hand, or to escape taxation, confiscation, or other real or imagined evils on the other. Europe and Canada own a lot of United States corporate stocks. The contrast is rather with bonds, where, prior to the imposition of the Interest Equalization Tax in 1963 which cut off the flow, foreign debtors would issue bonds in New York, but United States debtors would not issue bonds abroad to raise funds for expenditure in this country.

Direct investment may thus be capital movement, but it is more than that.

Control

Direct investment has long been defined as a capital movement involving continuing control by the investor. Sometimes this is put in legal terms, depending upon whether the equity ownership amounts to 10, 25, 48, 51, 95, or 100 percent of the foreign subsidiary. The 1968 mandatory restrictions on foreign direct investment, for

1. Jack N. Behrman, "Promoting Free World Economic Development Through Direct Investment," *American Economic Review*, *50*, No. 2 (May 1960), 271–81.

example, choose 10 percent as the criterion. To the economist, of course, the test is not the extent of ownership, but the locus of decision-making power. It is said that one 100 percent British-owned subsidiary of an American company has carried decentralized decision-making so far that it tells its parent, rather than asks it, even on the focal issues of dividends, capital budgeting, new products, research, and top personnel appointments, which decentralized corporations ordinarily reserve for centralized decision. If this is true, it is no different from an ordinary portfolio investment.

The economist, moreover, is interested in control only insofar as it affects behavior. In their study, *Canadian-United States Economic Relations,* Irving Brecher and S. S. Reisman are inclined to deprecate the importance of United States direct investment in Canada.[2] They argue that two companies, one foreign, one Canadian, operating in the same circumstances, both presumably rational and both seeking to maximize earnings, will operate in the same way. Things equal to the same thing are equal to each other. But a Canadian corporation and a foreign corporation in the same industry in Canada, even if both are unaffected by government, are not necessarily the same thing. If the Canadian corporation were an international firm of the same size and extent as the foreign, this might be so. For a company of a given volume and structure of assets and earnings it would make little difference economically whether the ownership were Canadian or United States. But assume that the Canadian is a national and the American an international corporation. They will scan different horizons in space, and possibly in time, and maximize different ob-

2. Ottawa, Queen's Printer, 1957.

jective functions. The international corporation may take depreciation allowances out of Canada to invest in a cheaper new source of output, whereas the Canadian firm's choice would be between expanding production in Canada or not expanding at all. Or in the event of world depression, the international corporation might cut back production in its various locations on the basis of the grief it foresaw from various national institutions—governments, unions, public opinion—rather than cutting back high-cost units first so as to equalize the marginal cost of production in each operation. With a narrower spatial and a shorter time horizon, the Canadian firm, because it is national and smaller, maximizes income in a Canadian context in the short run, the international firm in a world context in the long run. They may well then behave differently.

The control aspect of direct investment, which economists have been inclined to dismiss, is increasingly assuming political significance. In part this is the result of an unresolved conflict in international law; in part the result of what we may loosely characterize as pure nationalism. On the first score, for example, the United States assumes that it has the right to require parent companies to direct the operations of their subsidiaries in ways that conform to American purposes, while foreign governments, sovereign over the territory where these subsidiaries are located, deny the existence of such a right. What I have called pure nationalism is the uneasiness that many people instinctively have when they contemplate the fact that the activities of institutions within their economy and polity are "controlled" from outside the political unit. I shall argue that this feeling, like so many of the instincts direct investment or the international corporation arouses over the globe, is not to be trusted. The international corporation should be judged by how it operates, not for what it is. Scratch any of us deeply enough and you will find instincts of nationalism or xenophobia, overlain though they may be with layers of civilizing repression, and equally, instincts of peasant attachment to the soil; also populist fear of outside capital, mercantilist pleasure in expanding exports, on which I expatiate below, and perhaps others. The reactions are understandable, but they are not on that account to be approved.

The political, as distinct from the economic and legal, issue of control is thus made up of two elements, one involving attempts by governments to achieve national purposes through international corporations with headquarters in their jurisdictions and of other countries to resist them, and one of what I have called pure nationalism. It will be difficult to keep them distinct.

Growth of the Firm

There is a variety of theories about the firm, but the essence, at least in a number of theories, is growth. Firms manage and allocate resources; they innovate in new products; they are legal people; but primarily they grow. In growing they may well go abroad; in going abroad, they grow abroad.

In one formulation associated with the reinvestment of earnings, this comes close to a gambling theory of foreign investment. It has been observed that roughly half the earnings on foreign investment are reinvested abroad. From this a decision rule is deduced that firms bring home half their winnings and plow back the other half.[3]

3. E. R. Barlow and J. T. Wender, *Foreign Investment and Taxation* (Englewood Cliffs, N.J., Prentice-Hall, 1955).

The fact that there is an average reinvestment of half of their foreign earnings by United States companies cannot be doubted, but the existence of a rule of thumb that ascribes such conduct to individual corporations can be. A rule of thumb makes sense only when the benefits from its adoption in the reduction of costs of decision-making exceed the possible losses in poor investment choice. It is hard to believe that any firm is so irrational as to invest abroad by rule of thumb. [4]

Reinvest they do, when they have both profits and prospects for further profits. [5] The rate of reinvestment evidently depends on both profits and profitability. Nor is there any basis for suggesting that new investment is limited, after the initial start, to profits on past investment, on some sort of compound-interest formula. Investment goes forward on the basis of past earnings, new funds from the parent company, and new borrowings at home and especially abroad.

Within the total view that direct investment is a function of the growth of the firm are two strands, one emphasizing the market, the other the internal source of finance. The first is very much in vogue among business men. Direct investment, they say, is stimulated not by profits but by markets. Not only separate business spokesmen, like Mr. Richard Fenton formerly of Pfizer Inter-

---

4. For another rule of thumb, see Jean-Jacques Servan-Schreiber, who quotes a survey by a company named Donaldson and Lufkin which says that United States business considers it normal to invest 20 to 30 percent of its assets in Europe (*The American Challenge* [New York, Atheneum, 1968], p. 11). But the variance around such numbers, even if they should be valid averages, is so wide as to make the statement of little interest.

5. E. T. Penrose, "Foreign Investment and the Growth of the Firm," *Economic Journal, 66* (June 1956), 220–35.

national, but the business community as a whole, as recorded in the questionnaires of the National Industrial
Conference Board, insist that business investments seek
markets.[6] From markets a firm can imply a market share,
a volume of sales, and an earnings-to-sales ratio. A senior
executive is quoted as saying: "If we can look forward
to a certain *level of sales* we won't hesitate to invest, for
our profit will justify any amount of investment needed
to support an operation."[7] It is easy, of course, to find
counterexamples, where companies have a large foreign
market supplied by exports, and with investment limited
to distribution facilities and inventories, if any investment is needed at all. An outstanding example is the
Volkswagen company which enjoys substantial sales in
the United States, but deliberately refrains from domestic
manufacture, having in fact first bought and then sold a
former Studebaker plant at Linden, New Jersey. But the
explanations which businessmen give of their thought
processes must not be taken with literal seriousness. Like
Monsieur Jourdain in Molière's *Le Bourgeois Gentil-
homme* who spoke prose all his life without having been
aware of it, they doubtless maximize profits rather than
merely follow markets.

One factor accounting for the gap between business
behavior and business perception of it may be the initial
lag between investment and profits, resulting from
"breaking-in" or "teething" troubles. A chemical firm
established overseas for forty years found that its pre-

6. Judd Polk, Irene W. Meister, and Lawrence A. Veit, *U.S. Production Abroad and the Balance of Payments: A Survey of Corporate Investment Experience* (New York, National Industrial Conference Board, 1966), Chapter 4.

7. Ibid., p. 67. Italics in original.

World War II investment, which accounted for 42.5 percent of overseas assets, produced 53.5 percent of total earnings and 82 percent of dividends.[8] Subsequent investments are putatively as profitable as the earlier, with a time profile for earnings which starts low, or even negative, and rises to a normal long-run rate after a considerable interval. But the terrible possibility must be considered that businessmen actually do as they say they do and invest where markets are, without sufficiently considering long-run profits margins. The troubles of Chrysler with Rootes and Simca and of General Electric with Machines Bull in French computers raise the specter of such an outcome. But the returns are far from in.

Linking direct investment to markets and market position leads to an organic view of the process, as opposed to what we might call a mechanical one. The issue arises in connection with balance-of-payments restrictions, discussed in the next lecture. But the theory is clear. Direct investment is tied to markets. If markets grow, the firm must grow. If the firm stops growing, it dies. Anything that interferes with the growth of the firm, such as balance-of-payments restrictions, while the organic life of the market goes its way will kill the firm. But the issue can wait.

The second view connects direct investment not with

8. From a master's thesis at M.I.T. by G. V. Lydecker, "Direct Foreign Investment and the Balance of Payments: A Study of the President's Program of Voluntary Restraint" (1966), p. 106.

Another company (ibid., p. 98) stated that the bulk of its dividends came from the mature investments "as would be expected."

See also "Cummins Trimming Ventures in Europe," *New York Times* (January 22, 1968), which states that losses to date are about $8.4 million on $17 million invested in three plants in Britain, one opened in 1957 and two in 1966.

markets but with the cost of capital to the firm. Many economists regard retained earnings as not only cheaper capital than borrowings or the sale of new equities, but so cheap as to approach a negative cost. Extra dividends for stockholders only lead them to expect more. So long as there is any reasonable basis for expansion, the firm should reinvest rather than pay out profits above some long-run, and very slowly rising, amount. In addition, ploughed-back earnings escape the personal income tax and can be cashed in, if need be, at the lower rates on capital gains. If opportunities for growth at home are limited, look abroad. In any event, grow.

There is something to this doctrine, but how much cannot be tested quantitatively with current Department of Commerce data, which lump open-book claims with equity as "direct investment." In 1957, when the latest published survey of United States foreign investment was undertaken, foreign sources of capital provided 40 percent of total assets, largely in debt, and 25 percent of the total debt financing was furnished from the United States. Since 1957, however, and especially since 1963, United States companies have been borrowing in the Euro-bond market and the Euro-dollar market at rates of interest that may be small compared with expected profit possibilities and with the rates at which European companies borrow but are high by United States capital market standards. Direct investment involves much more than the reinvestment of funds that United States business is reluctant to distribute to shareholders. Firms grow, and may grow abroad rather than at home for one reason or another, but direct investment involves entering into commitments and taking risks, not merely investing earnings for which no better use is handy.

Monopolistic Competition

Each of these explanations—capital movement pack-aged with decision-making and associated with tech-nology, former of capital, consequence of the growth of the firm—has an element of the truth but none provides an entirely satisfactory explanation of the phenomenon. The United States government is currently fostering di-rect investment while seeking to limit the capital out-flow involved. The thesis that asserts firms are irrational and invest as if they were gambling is hardly persuasive, possibly not a priori, but at least in a Darwinian sense. As long as some foreign markets continue to be served by imports, as well as by production near the market, the notion that direct investment is a function of markets alone is unconvincing. Control may lie at the root of the problem presented by direct investment, but why do some firms want to control and not others?

A more general theory—originally propounded in a thesis at the Massachusetts Institute of Technology by Stephen H. Hymer—is that direct investment belongs more to the theory of industrial organization than to the theory of international capital movements.[9] The invest-ing company can earn a higher rate of return abroad than at home—as it must if it undertakes the risks and over-comes the costs of operating in a different political and legal environment, at a distance from its decision-making center. It is not enough for the return to be higher abroad than at home. If this were all, capital would move through organized capital markets rather than through

9. Stephen H. Hymer, "The International Operations of Na-tional Firms: A Study of Direct Investment" (doctoral dissertation, Cambridge, Mass., M.I.T., 1960).

firms that specialize in the production and distribution of goods. Capital markets specialize in moving capital, and under competitive conditions they are better
at it than firms engaged in other lines. In addition to
earning more abroad than at home, the investing firm
must be able to earn a higher return in the market where
it is investing than local firms earn. There are costs of
operating at a distance, costs not only of travel, communication, and time lost in communicating information and decisions, but also costs of misunderstanding
that leads to errors.[10] For a firm to undertake direct investment in a foreign country it must have an advantage
over existing or potentially competitive firms in that
country. If not, those firms, operating more cheaply in
other respects because nearer the locus of decision-making
and without the filter of long lines to distort communication, would put the intruder out of business. One is
tempted to say that foreign firms which specialize in
market-oriented products will be able successfully to establish subsidiaries in a country that does not produce
the goods. But this is not so unless the firms possess some
advantage which they can transfer from one country to

10. Answering a question at a business conference, a banker
stated: "Most American companies expect and do get a higher return on their capital abroad than they do in the U.S. This is
justified if only because the risk of investment outside your own
country is greater. This is not so much a political risk in Europe
as the risk of not being able to see business opportunities as clearly
as the local company." See E. Russell Eggers, Manager, The Chase
Manhattan Bank, Paris, "The Pattern of American Investment in
Europe," Record of Proceedings Second International Investment
Symposium, New College, Oxford, July 1964, in *The Changing
World* (London, P. N. Kemp-Gee, 1965), p. 287. For this last risk,
of course, it is necessary to have a higher original rate of return
than foreign, not domestic, companies.

another but which cannot be acquired by local firms. With perfect international markets for technology, management, labor skills, components, and other material input, the market abroad will be served by a local firm.

Put the matter another way: in a world of perfect competition for goods and factors, direct investment cannot exist. In these conditions, domestic firms would have an advantage over foreign firms in the proximity of their operations to their decision-making centers, so that no firm could survive in foreign operation. For direct investment to thrive there must be some imperfection in markets for goods or factors, including among the latter technology, or some interference in competition by government or by firms, which separates markets.

This theory may be illustrated by contrasting it with another. In their interesting *Federal Tax Treatment of Foreign Income,* Krause and Dam assert: "Another reason for investing abroad is that production costs may be lower than in the United States because of favorable wage rates, raw material prices, or interest rates . . . or because of the opportunity to reduce transportation costs, distribution costs, inventory and servicing costs to the markets for which the outputs are intended."[11] In the present view, cheaper costs abroad than at home are not enough. What must be explained is why the production abroad is not undertaken by local entrepreneurs, who have an inherent advantage over outside investors. There must be a more than compensating advantage on the part of the foreigner before direct investment will be called forth.

The nature of the monopolistic advantages which pro-

11. Lawrence B. Krause and Kenneth W. Dam, *Federal Tax Treatment of Foreign Income* (Washington, D.C., The Brookings Institution, 1964), p. 64.

duce direct investment can be indicated under a variety of headings:

1. departures from perfect competition in goods markets, including product differentiation, special marketing skills, retail price maintenance, administered pricing, and so forth;

2. departures from perfect competition in factor markets, including the existence of patented or unavailable technology, of discrimination in access to capital, of differences in skills of managers organized into firms rather than hired in competitive markets;

3. internal and external economies of scale, the latter being taken advantage of by vertical integration;

4. government limitations on output or entry.

It may be useful to illustrate these separate advantages briefly.

Goods Markets

That product differentiation breeds direct investment is indicated by its prevalence in branded products such as pharmaceuticals, cosmetics, soft drinks, and specialty foodstuffs, and in concentrated industries such as automobiles, tires, chemicals, electrical appliances, electronic components, farm machinery, office equipment. It does not occur in standardized goods produced by competitive industries such as textiles, clothing, flour milling, and distribution (except for Sears, Roebuck in Latin America). In oligopolistic industries there is likely to be two-way investment, with Lever Brothers and Royal Dutch Shell in the United States and Procter and Gamble, Esso, and other United States oil companies in Britain, or

Campbell Soup and Heinz in Europe and Knorr and Nestlé in the United States. Indeed, in concentrated industries there is pressure for each firm to develop a position in each important or potentially important market —regardless of the rate of profit obtainable in absolute terms—to prevent any of its few competitors from obtaining a substantial advantage which it could put to use over a wider area. The threat of competition by a foreign firm in the home market may be reduced if the domestic firm stands ready to retaliate through an existing subsidiary in the market of the threatener. A major drug company is said to admit that it loses on its investment in Brazil but has to be there to cover the actions of the competition.

Marketing skill was what brought one of the earliest types of United States investment—life insurance—to Europe and is what Americans and Europeans alike believe is the major contribution of many American companies today. It is closely associated, of course, with product differentiation through advertising and with administered pricing (though European competitors complain of price cutting). Incidentally, the experience of the life insurance companies supports the theory that direct investment is based on an advantage of one kind or another and is impossible where such advantage does not exist. United States companies taught their marketing secrets to European insurance companies and then withdrew to the confines of this country. Theories that rely on the growth of the firm have little explanation for withdrawal. Servan-Schreiber states, "United States troops will leave Vietnam, but United States industry will not leave Europe."[12] Hymer, on whose theory this

12. *The American Challenge*, p. 275.

analysis relies, puts it colorfully: "Corporations do not die like ordinary trees; they are like California red-woods."[13] But these pronouncements do not take account of some failures, such as those American companies which tried to introduce cake mixes and bowling into Europe in the last decade, or of withdrawals other than that of the life insurance companies—General Electric, Rexall (Boots drug), and Woolworth—from Britain at the end of the 1930s.

Factor Markets

Superiority of management may be the advantage that many companies bring to foreign investment, though it usually must be combined with monopoly advantages in goods markets or increasing returns to scale to convert it into a basis for operating in foreign markets. The nature of that superiority is elusive, being said variously to consist in centralization of decision-making and in decentralization, in scientific cost-benefit analysis and in merely a concern for marketing, in the maintenance of high standards on technical performance, tolerances, delivery dates, and so on, at the same time that it runs afoul of local practices and especially of trade union tradition. These aspects of the problem will be developed in subsequent lectures.

There is little or no advantage to the foreign investor in access to labor other than management and technical staff.

The advantage of the large international company in

13. In an unpublished memorandum, which he kindly made available to me.

raising capital is another topic that arises in specific contexts later.

This leaves us, at this stage of the proceedings, to discuss patents and industrial secrets, which are a major advantage of the large international corporation in differentiated products. Patents and restricted technology limit entry. The question that inevitably arises, however, is whether to exploit the advantage through licensing foreign firms or to undertake foreign production oneself. Examples can be found of each—and in the same industry. St. Gobain, a French company, developed a new process for producing plate glass and undertook to build a plant in Tennessee, which was called upon its completion "the most modern obsolete plant in the world." The reason for this obsolescence was that the British Pilkington company developed a newer and superior method of producing plate glass, the float process. But rather than undertake production in the United States Pilkington decided to license existing producers—Pittsburgh Plate Glass, Libby-Owens-Ford, and the Ford Motor Company. The choice was presumably made on the basis of fine calculations of costs and prospective profits. A further factor seems to have been that the Pilkington company is a family concern which hesitated to borrow enough capital to start production on the scale necessary to compete with the three American companies (which requires a full line of automotive glass products) and which perhaps was concerned that it would let loose the demon of cut-throat oligopolistic competition.

If we assume that a firm is not constrained by unwillingness to raise capital or by fear of the consequences of breaking into a foreign market, what will the choice between licensing and direct investment depend on? Where the license fee fails to capture the full rent inherent in technical superiority, the advantage lies in direct investment. There may be other considerations: whether the patent or industrial secret is adequately protected by the license, or whether at the expiration of the arrangement the licenser will find his secret gone; whether the licensee is likely to provide competition in other markets—possibilities which it might be illegal to protect against through agreement but which are safeguarded through ownership. Research is needed to amass a series of cases in which the choice between licensing and direct investment has been made in one sense or the other, in order to formulate exactly the nature of the governing considerations. Since both methods are used, however, it is evident that the calculation is a close one. Licenses tend to bring in a lower return, directly and indirectly, but are less expensive in capital, time, and energy.

One apparently irrational feature of the choice appears in statements gathered by interview from two American firms that they are willing to enter into joint ventures with foreign participants if the foreigners provide some advantage in kind—technical knowledge, marketing skills, or "some other valuable and unique service"—but not otherwise.[14] The irrationality, to which we return, is that admission of local participants to the equity of a foreign investment should be a function of the price they pay, not the character of the payment. If the local capitalists pay a high enough price for a small enough portion of the equity, money is as good as real considerations, or better. The higher the price the greater the extent to which the foreign investor capitalizes the advantage, or a portion of it, that he brings to the venture, rather than drawing an income from it.

14. Lydecker, pp. 98, 112.

Economies of Scale

Economies of scale are very much in people's minds today in Europe where attention is focused on the large size of American companies compared with the relatively small size of European concerns. The advantages of large-scale production internal to the firm are self-evident, although it is useful to point out that there are counter-balancing diseconomies of scale in administration, which at some point, different in different industries and for different methods of management, set limits to the optimum scale of operations. Long-term cost curves turn up somewhere, or competition would reduce the number of firms in each industry to one.

Economies of scale must be distinguished from the profits available through horizontal integration which extends to the point where the firm has some control over price. The benefit to the firm from extending operations overseas may lie not in producing greater numbers at a cheaper cost per unit, but in raising the price at which units are sold. When this occurs, direct investment involves a loss for the world, though perhaps a gain for a country. Production is reduced rather than expanded, and price is raised above marginal cost, which remains at least as high as before. In the short run, the direct investment that obtains a larger share of the market and market power may be equally profitable—no more, no less—than the direct investment that lowers cost through internal economies of scale achieved through horizontal integration. In the long run, however, monopoly profits persist, whereas in the competitive situation profits return to the long-run level.

While internal economies of scale—and monopoly—account for horizontal integration, external economies of

scale lead to vertical integration. In a number of lines
where production is bulky, inventories are expensive, and
coordination of decision is required at several stages of
the process, the firm may be a better means of organizing
production than the competitive market. In oil, for example, it is possible for separate firms to produce crude
petroleum, transport it, refine it, and market the products, dealing with each other at arm's length through
markets. But there are substantial economies, it appears,
in coordinating decisions at various stages of production,
so much so that direct investment in the petroleum industry is the rule, both backward to sources of crude
petroleum supplies and forward to consumer markets for
refined products. In some industries, such as metals, vertical integration goes only to the source of raw materials.
Steel companies own iron mines, copper companies produce copper ore abroad, aluminum companies own baux-
ite (and electricity), so that they may better coordinate
the output and shipment of ore with the needs of metal
refining. Their advantage over other firms with equal
technology, managerial skill, access to capital, and so on
is that they coordinate mining operations with transport
and marketing—with an eye to minimizing both inter-
ruptions in flows and the piling up of unwieldy inventories. Like governmental planning in Rosenstein-
Rodan's 1943 article on balanced growth, vertical integration converts external economies to internal profits.[15]
But the capital needed for operations on this scale tends
to limit entry into these industries, and to provide at
least the possibility of oligopoly which raises price above
marginal cost. And the existence of separate stages of pro-

15. P. N. Rosenstein-Rodan, "Problems of Industrialization of
Eastern and South-eastern Europe," Economic Journal, 53 (June-
September 1943).

duction in different countries within the same company gives rise to problems of transfer pricing, discussed below.

Vertical integration can also serve an economic purpose in helping to avoid the risks of technological change or new channels of trade, which require coordinated new investments at various stages of the movement of a commodity from production to consumption. I became aware of this in studying the economic history of Britain, noting that tenant farmers found it difficult to shift from wheat to dairy products because of the difficulty of dividing the risks of investment, and the profits, between the owners of East Anglian farms and their tenant-operators, or that the failure to change from small coal cars on the British railways to larger, more efficient ones was because the cars were owned by the coal mines but new investment by both the mines and the railroads was needed to arrive at the new size. A current illustration given by my colleague, Morris Adelman, is the profitability of large new investments—in coal mines, railroad cars, and loading facilities in the United States, large ships and unloading and distribution equipment in Europe—to bring West Virginia coal to Europe at half the cost that coal can be mined there. It proves impossible to undertake the investments needed at each stage of the process without vertical integration which would coordinate it.

Vertical integration can also be a pathological condition. Competition, like matter and games, is subject to entropy. Even where there are no economic advantages in coordinating production at various stages, or of coordinating new investments at different levels of production to carry through innovation, companies may feel safer with assured access to sources of inputs and to outlets for products. In these circumstances the industry will shift from numerous firms which are small and competitive at each stage to one of a few large, vertically integrated concerns. Once started, the process acquires momentum. When the oil company that used to sell gas feed stocks to petrochemical companies acquires a petrochemical subsidiary of its own, other chemical firms it used to supply feel constrained to acquire their own sources of supply. A striking example is the purchase by Alcan Aluminium Limited of Canada of a half interest in the government-owned Aardal og Sunndal Verk (A.S.V.) aluminum smelter in Norway, a move that expanded the former's "aluminum capacity by almost 20 percent and eliminated a source of price competition that had vexed the entire industry."[16] Alcan's interest in acquiring A.S.V.—to reduce competition—is made evident in this remark. But the newspaper account goes on to indicate that the Norwegian government felt that A.S.V. needed a tie-up with a producer of alumina to assure future deliveries. "Norway feared that the trend toward integrated production . . . might leave a lone smelter without supplies or customers."[17] In some industries, such as automobiles, vertical integration proves inefficient in the long run, and the industry proceeds to disintegration and the establishment of separate firms for component manufacture which deal at arm's length. The Cummins Engine Company of Indiana sought to obtain a foothold in the diesel-engine industry in Europe but found itself unable to develop markets since truck producers in Europe (Fiat, Berliet, Mercedes) all produced their own diesel engines—a stage in the development of truck production regarded as behind the disintegrated structure of the United States and

16. "Alcan Aluminium Active in Norway," *New York Times* (March 31, 1967).
17. Ibid.

Britain.[18] Vertical integration can thus either make for direct investment reducing competition in goods markets and the markets for inputs, or it can frustrate direct investment.

A special form of imperfectly competitive market for factors is in capital. I have claimed that direct investment does not represent a capital movement, and this is largely true. But on occasion, in industries that need large amounts of capital, a foreign firm will have an advantage over a domestic firm because of its superior credit standing. The international capital market is not perfect, and even to the extent that capital markets are joined, different rates are charged to borrowers of different credit standing. Many borrowers cannot command the large sums necessary for capital-intensive investments at all. I do not mean to limit this to access to the New York capital market or the Euro-dollar bond market. Even before the restraints on United States investment abroad, United States firms were borrowing abroad despite higher nominal interest rates: in case of difficulty, the asset and the liability would be in the same currency basket and the net risk of loss thereby diminished. Since the restrictions, the propensity to borrow abroad has increased. And not only in New York and in Euro-dollars but abroad and in foreign currencies, American firms of worldwide credit standing typically have an advantage over domestic firms with only a national credit rating and limited liquidity. In some countries, foreign capital markets are particularly underdeveloped, and capital must be brought from the United States or transferred from one foreign operation to another. But this is not the essense of direct investment. With perfect capital markets,

18. "Cummins Trimming Ventures in Europe."

and assuming the borrowers are of equal credit standing, the domestic entrepreneur abroad could borrow in New York as easily as the American entrepreneur. The fact is that where the direct investor has an advantage over his local competition based on capital availability, this is the result not of his nationality, but of his better credit rating in all parts of the international capital market. Whatever the source of capital, the international firm with its large cash flow and high liquidity is a better credit risk than local enterprise and, in imperfectly competitive markets, gets lower rates on loans and preferred access to limited funds.

Let me present the pith of this theory of direct investment with the use of the simple formula for capitalizing a stream of income, $C = \dfrac{I}{r}$ where C is the value of a capital asset, I is the stream of income it produces, and r is the rate of return on investment. Thus, for example, an investment producing a $5 flow of income is worth $100 at a 5 percent rate of profit. This theory of direct investment insists that ordinary capital movements take place between countries when interest rates differ, but that direct investment corresponds for the most part to differences in I that can be earned by entrepreneurs from abroad over local entrepreneurs. I is higher for the foreigner than for the local entrepreneur because of some advantage in goods markets such as a differentiated product or assured outlets or marketing skill; in factor markets, such as specialized technology or management skill; or in both goods and factor markets through coordinating operations at several stages of production. When the advantage in factor markets is access to cheap capital, because of either the larger cash flow of depreciation and profits in internal funds or a preferred position in capital markets as a borrower, differences in r may contribute to the result. Primarily, however, the theory asserts that direct investment occurs when the foreign firm can earn a higher I than the local firm, whereas ordinary capital movements reflect a lower r. The exception for imperfect capital markets will be developed later. The theory can be illustrated with the far from hypothetical example of a European family seeking to sell out a family firm. A foreign firm, typically from the United States, is able to bid more for the going concern than its European competitors, i.e. pay a higher C, not because of a lower r—or perhaps better not solely, or even mainly because of a lower r—but because it can earn a higher I on the firm's assets.

Government

Finally government. The role of government does not affect the choice between local and foreign firms, except when it refuses to sanction direct investment. If we assume that foreign firms have an advantage over local firms, the question is whether the goods are provided by imports or by a direct investor. Here government enters with tariffs. Government may impose a tariff in the hope of stimulating production by nationals, only to find that it has encouraged the entry of foreign firms.

Brash, for example, claims that increases in tariffs have been decisive in stimulating American investment in Australian manufacturing industry.[19] This statement can be broken down into two stages. Australian tariffs stimulate investment behind the tariff walls. The advantages of American manufacturing concerns over Aus-

19. Donald T. Brash, *American Investment in Australian Industry* (Cambridge, Mass., Harvard University Press, 1965), p. 40.

tralian firms result in the entry into Australian manufacturing of American rather than Australian firms. The
same stimulation to direct investment presumably came
from the formation of the European Economic Community, and again in two stages. The formation of the
customs union favored firms inside the common tariff
over those outside. Foreign firms that were discriminated
against by the customs union set up subsidiaries within
the customs area if they had an advantage that enabled
them to compete successfully with local firms.

Government intervention to cut off imports and substitute domestic production may lead foreign firms into
what has been called "defensive investment," i.e. investment that produces a less than average return, but where
the difference between the gross return plus and the loss
that would have resulted from exclusion gives the necessary rate of return on a marginal basis.[20] A firm threat-
ened with a loss of 4 percent a year on an existing investment may find it worthwhile to undertake new investment at a below-average return to prevent the loss. The
behavior is viable in the short, but not of course in the
long run, when all costs are variable and average costs
become marginal costs.

In my judgment, however, the major impact of the
Treaty of Rome was not to create new opportunities for
outside firms to invest within the Community or to
threaten exporters with losses against which they sought
to defend. More significant, I think, was the treaty's calling attention to opportunities for profitable investment
which had until then been ignored. Europe had lain
over the horizon of most American companies, out of
sight. Opportunities for profitable investment existed,

20. A. Lamfalussy, *Investment and Growth in Mature Economies*
(Oxford, Blackwell, 1963).

but company managements in the United States were unaware of them. Coming as it did when major domestic postwar investment programs had been completed, the Rome treaty, plus its forerunner, the European Coal and Steel Community, and successive steps toward integration which followed it, had little importance in altering the bases on which close calculations of alternative profit opportunities were made. What they did was to lift the attention of United States business to a wider horizon and to focus interest on the fast-growing European market with its unfolding investment opportunities. Government's role was minimal. The major stimulus to direct investment in Europe in the late 1950s and the 1960s was a discontinuous enlargement in the horizon scanned by United States corporate management. The Common Market may have triggered it. It did not produce it.[21]

Corollaries of the Monopolistic Theory of Direct Investment

The fact that the foreign corporation has some advantage over the local corporation, which makes direct investment possible, has a number of corollaries. It is a strong reason in the eyes of the investor against sharing his equity. The world of affairs abounds in the apparently reasonable suggestion that the overseas investor enter into joint ventures with local interests. Instead of buying 100 percent of a domestic firm, buy half. But the overseas investor asks why he should give half the scarcity

21. For a demonstration that the tariff was less of a stimulus to U.S. investment in the European Economic Community than industrial growth there, though the effects were additive rather than mutually exclusive, see Lawrence B. Krause, *European Economic Integration and the United States* (Washington, D.C., The Brookings Institution, 1968), pp. 126–31.

value of his advantage away. This reasoning assumes, as I have indicated, that there are barriers to adjusting the price paid for half the enterprise which would enable the foreign investor to capitalize on the scarcity value of his contribution. It may be difficult for the local investor to appreciate the profitability of the prospective enterprise, so that he would be unwilling to make his monetary contribution at an implicit valuation of the foreign contribution which accorded with the foreigner's view. To an economist, as I have said, the problem has an air of irrationality or imperfect knowledge about it. In a broad market there should be no difficulty in varying the price of the foreign contribution of a special advantage such as technology, relative to the domestic contribution of money, land, facilities, or whatever is involved, so as to represent something like its market real scarcity value.

There is, of course, one other aspect to a foreign investor's reluctance to share control, or even to tolerate a substantial interest, and in many cases it may be the controlling one. The interests of the partners may differ. The foreign investor may wish to accumulate capital, whereas the domestic investor wants dividends. In this case they would disagree on the appropriate rate of reinvestment of profits, or in readiness to undertake new investments to make good losses or to take advantage of new opportunities. Thus Heinz bought a higher share of its Japanese subsidiary after its partners in that country were reluctant to expand at the rate they thought was required; and Coca-Cola found it difficult to persuade its partner bottlers abroad to undertake the necessary investment to move from 6-ounce to 10- and 12-ounce bottles. Or the international corporation may have a wide number of interests, in a variety of countries, which are related to its interest in a particular subsidiary, while the partner in that subsidiary has only one. The most usual source of a conflict of interest arises where the international corporation is integrated over a number of stages of production and the local subsidiary covers one. How intercompany transactions are priced may become a bone of contention in this case, as it affects whether profits are earned in the wholly owned parent or the partially owned child. Transfer pricing is an important question for that other partner of every company in every country, the tax collector, who clearly has an interest in ensuring that profits are earned and taxed in the jurisdiction where they ought to be.[22]

The economic answer to the tax collector is easy to formulate, difficult to apply. Payments for all goods and services sold within a corporation, including rents, royalties, and fees for patents, industrial knowledge, and management services, should be set at the prices that would prevail in a competitive market, with all element of monopoly or monopsony eliminated. In the well-known case of oil tanker charges, however, one must be careful not to apply the single-voyage charter rates, which are highly competitive but cover such a small part of the market that they tend to fluctuate in exaggerated fashion as changes in total demand and supply are brought to bear against a limited segment of the market. In this and similar cases, some other criterion must be used. The market for short- and long-term charters is competitive, so that it is relatively easy to get a good approximation to a short- or long-term price which would be reached with competitive arm's-length bargaining. In the crude oil market, which is very imperfect and where actual

22. See James A. Shulman, "Transfer Pricing in Multinational Business" (doctoral dissertation, Cambridge, Mass., Harvard Graduate School of Business Administration, August 1966).

transactions are known only to a limited degree, it is perhaps possible to calculate a proxy competitive price. But in highly complex mechanical, chemical, or electrical goods, such calculation becomes impossible since there is no market from which "competitive" prices can be estimated or approximated. Tax commissioners and private partners may be able in one way or another to "construct" a profit which makes crude legal or bargaining sense perhaps, but it is difficult to devise an economically justifiable criterion.

The answer given by the large international companies to the demand for local participation is hardly satisfactory. They urge the local investor to buy shares in the parent company. But the local investor wants a piece of the monopoly profits from the corporation's advantage in the local market, profits which, in the nature of direct investment, are higher than those in the main place of business.

Where takeovers occur, or a minority shareholding is bought out, as in the Ford of Dagenham minority purchase in 1960, the local owner of assets or shareholder can capitalize a portion of the prospective gains by selling his assets for more than they are worth to him or to his countrymen. When Ford of Detroit offered the 40 percent minority shareholders of the British company 145 shillings a share, the market quotation was in the low 90s, and the local shareholder got a capital gain of more than 50 percent. Ford of Detroit, which had more than $1 billion in idle cash in the home office and which anticipated no better use for it than buying up the remaining interest in its already controlled but prospectively profitable British subsidiary, was willing—or, perhaps it should be said, was obliged—to share the anticipated profits to a considerable extent in order to acquire the shareholding.

International corporations thus prefer 100 percent ownership to joint ventures or minority holdings. To the extent that they need additional finance, they seek it abroad, and through debt. This is to limit risk by holding assets and liabilities in the same currency and avoid the possibility of losing assets while liabilities remain. The reason for obtaining capital in debt form is to protect the company's equity. In 1957 United States firms owned 60 percent of the assets in their foreign subsidiaries, but this consisted of 85 percent of the equity capital and only 25 percent of the creditor capital. By subtraction, foreign investors had 15 percent of the equity and 75 percent of the debt. There are instances where United States corporations prefer to take a limited interest in foreign operations. The Kaiser company, for example, is said to limit itself to a 25 or 30 percent interest, wanting a voice in management, some earnings, but a quiet life. Again some governments, notably that of India, require foreign corporations, as a condition of entering the market, to undertake to sell as much as 30 percent of their equity to local investors. In these circumstances, the foreign investor naturally seeks to spread the stock widely so as to prevent the coalition of a strong minority voice in management. And, as we shall see in the fourth lecture, there have been strong measures proposed in Canada to get a substantial proportion of foreign equity in Canadian corporations into Canadian hands. But where the investment is based on an advantage over local competitors, and there are difficulties in getting the full capitalized value of this advantage in advance by selling it at its value to the holder, foreign equity owners may be expected to resist these pressures, quite apart from the complication of loss of control.

The second corollary is less evident. Direct investment

belongs to the theory of monopolistic competition. But
while direct investment may gobble up competitors and
exploit its monopolistic advantages, its main impact is in
widening the area of competition. Domestic markets are
protected, if not by tariffs, at least by distance, ignorance,
lethargy. The small, inefficient domestic producer is
typically more of a monopolist than the large, monopolistically competitive wide-ranging firm. Such a domestic
market thrives on high prices and low volume. Sometimes, as in France before the European Coal and Steel
Community and the European Economic Community,
a handful of large firms holds a high price umbrella each
over an entourage of small and inefficient coexisting or
symbiotic firms in the rest of the industry. The French
call this sort of market Malthusian.[23] Retail price maintenance, understandings that no firm will rock the boat,
"conscious parallel action" even if no explicit agreement
(to use the United States Supreme Court's phrase), make
the local market before the entry of the international
corporation much more monopolistic than the monopolistically competitive intruder. The cost advantages
of the intruder are so great, even when its conduct is not
aggressively competitive, that prices are reduced, volumes
are expanded, and the monopolistic phenomenon extends the area of competition.

A strong case against this competition can be based on
infant-industry argument. Given a chance to develop, to

23. As an interwar example of resistance to direct investment
based on fear of competition, see Alfred Sauvy, *Histoire économique
de la France entre les deux guerres* (Paris, Fayard, 1967), p. 372.
The Czech shoe company, B'ata, planned to construct a factory in
France. Immediately, the so-called Poullen Law of March 22, 1936,
was passed to forbid the opening of new factories or ateliers for
shoe manufacture, or the enlargement of existing ones.

acquire technology, penetrate markets, learn management skills, and so forth, national firms may grow to compete effectively with the large international firm, and it is useful to give them the chance. This is so not for nationalistic reasons or for sentiment, but for efficiency. This exception apart, however, the presumption is that the international firm, unregulated except where necessary to keep entry free, will lead to greater world economic efficiency. The small local firm will object to "unfair" competition; it is really objecting to competition. We recur to this theme in the last lecture on the international corporation, but it may be well to foreshadow the theme here.

The International Corporation and Efficiency

Compare the growth of the international corporation in the 1950s and 1960s with the rise of the national corporation in the 1880s and 1890s in the United States. There was great concern for abuses of competition, culminating in the passage of the Sherman Anti-Trust Act of 1890. Muckrakers inveighed against big business. Populists attacked the domination of Wall Street. But the national corporation, emerging out of the growth of the local corporation and the regional corporation, made an important contribution, over time, to economic efficiency in the United States. Prior to 1900, factor markets in the United States were less perfect than they are now. Wage rates were higher in the New England and Middle Atlantic states and the West than in the South and Middle West. Capital was cheaper in financial centers than in the rural areas of the West and South. Capital markets of New York, Philadelphia, Boston, Chicago, and the major cities were joined after a fashion, but the connections between them and the rest of the country were limited and fragile.

The rise of the national corporation provided a new institution alongside the imperfect factor markets, which worked toward factor-price equalization and economic efficiency. Where capital failed to move easily to other cities, national corporations established financial offices and raised capital in New York. Where labor failed to move to the high wage areas in the North and East, corporations brought capital to labor in the South and West. There were other pulls on national corporations than factor-price differences—pulls, moreover, that also worked toward efficiency by attracting corporations to sources of supply, thus saving transport costs on heavy materials, or by pulling them to the market, thus saving transport costs on bulky assembled products. But owing to the immobility of labor and land and to barriers to the free movement of capital, factor markets by themselves were inadequate to produce the efficient optimum implied by equality of factor prices. The national corporation provided an economic institution, unforeseen by the classical economists, which, while it carried the threat of monopoly, brought the United States closer to the classic competitive world. To achieve this result it may have been necessary to maintain a strong antitrust movement to ward off the evils of monopoly while moving toward the blessings of greater factor mobility.

The national corporation, it should be made clear, was a product of the railroad, telegraph, and telephone, which made it possible for a decision-making center to operate over wide distances without too great cost. The jet aircraft, the radio-telephone, and the rapid rate of growth in postwar Europe have lifted the horizons of many national corporations to the world scene, to join the limited number of pioneers who go back to 1900 and earlier. The development of corporations which scan the world for investment opportunities does offer the possibility, along with the spread of monopoly, of equalizing factor prices, even in the face of the international barriers to the movement of capital and of labor, in strictly analogous fashion to the rise of the national corporation in the United States after 1880.

Circumstances Alter Cases

If direct investment may expand or reduce competition it follows that it is impossible to draw general conclusions about its desirability, assuming that competition is desirable. It is necessary, rather, to settle matters on a case-by-case basis. This is not unknown in the antitrust field. In the United States prospective mergers are submitted to the Department of Justice to see whether the character of the firms, or their resultant size, is judged—case by case—to restrain trade. In Europe, it is claimed that business agreements, or cartels, are not objectionable in themselves, but that there are good cartels and bad cartels, just as there are permissible and impermissible mergers in the United States. This is an uncomfortable position for the law. The economist, on the other hand, has long been used to deriving different conclusions from the same action, depending upon whether other things were equal *(ceteris paribus)* or altered *(mutatis mutandis)*.

Equal treatment under the law requires the world to be indifferent to whether International Business Machines or the General Electric Company buys Machines Bull Compagnie, the French computer concern. But if I.B.M. were to acquire it, competition in the computer field would be reduced; for G.E. to team up with Machines Bull and Olivetti, on the other hand, or for Radio Corporation of America to join with Siemens, holds out the hope—although not, as it turned out, a very bright one—of widening the range of world competition in the computer field.

Direct investment is, then, a subject in which it is necessary to judge case by case, on the basis of the relevant circumstances, before coming to conclusions about the effects of one or another action. All the while countries, companies, and academic economists search for rules of thumb which can be generalized. "Investment for new enterprises, but not for takeovers"; or for "production, but not control"; or "in manufacturing, but not in distribution," and so forth. We shall encounter a variety of attempts to prescribe general precepts, and I will find it possible as a rule to suggest circumstances in which they are not appropriate.

The necessity for companies and countries to proceed case-by-case, depending upon circumstances, is not only offensive to Anglo-Saxon notions of jurisprudence; administrative discretion raises the possibility of rapid changes in rules of conduct and of arbitrary disagreements between countries. The beauty of the market, as economists extol it, is that it operates through the direction of the invisible hand. When the French government changes its mind three times in five years on general rules for foreign investment and ends up with administrative discretion lacking procedures for appeal or even for pushing for decision, the directing hand is painfully visible. Moreover, two hands, attached to two different countries, may push in different directions, letting the international company slide between them in one case, or punishing it doubly in another. But more on these issues below.

United States Concern with Direct Investment

The bulk of this book deals with the concern of foreign countries about international firms, largely but not entirely companies owned in the United States. But it must not be overlooked that the United States has an interest in direct investment abroad by American firms. This interest may not be exactly what it is pictured to be by some shades of opinion at home and abroad which regard American companies, and the government and people of the United States, as bent upon the ruthless economic and political domination and exploitation of the rest of the world. It nevertheless exists.

We can safely neglect the possible concern of the United States about foreign corporations in the United States. During World War II, many people and the government were worried about German corporations which were thought to be engaged in spying and sabotage, much as American firms are occasionally accused of working for the operations branch of the C.I.A., or identified with the machinations of "imperial warmongers" in sensitized areas today. The United States government operated an Alien Property Custodian to root out the tentacles of German infiltration through General Aniline and Film Corporation, the Bausch and Lomb subsidiary of Zeiss, and others. A large Safehaven program was built to attack German penetration of Allied and neutral countries. It goes without saying that most of the concern was highly emotional and nationalistic, just as most if

not all of today's fears about American political and
military penetration by economic means are unfounded.
During the war the United States Treasury required the
British government to acquire and dispose of British-
owned shares of the American Viscose Corporation as an
earnest of its readiness to turn its pockets inside out,
in a sort of means test, before qualifying for Lend-Lease
assistance. Apart from these rather inaesthetic wartime
episodes, however, the United States is disposed to give
foreign business full national treatment—carte blanche
on the basis of equality with domestic companies to set
up business in this country under the laws of some state
and of the country, to make profits, and to pay taxes.

United States interest in American investments abroad
can conveniently be treated under five headings: political
and military, taxation, balance of payments, and antitrust, which relate to the national interest, and those of
groups such as capital and labor within the totality. This
is by no means a complete catalogue of the possible concerns, but it covers the main items. The national and
parochial interests, it should be noted, lie as often as not
in restricting rather than promoting direct investment
by United States companies. The lecture returns to a
consideration of the view that direct investment is a plot
by the United States to dominate the world.

Political and Military

One of the earliest post-World War II actions affecting
United States overseas investment of which I am aware,
and with which I was concerned, was the moratorium on
new investment in Germany imposed in 1945. Its purpose
was clearly political, and perhaps counter-productive in
an economic sense. The Department of State was charged

with keeping Germany disarmed, getting it denazified, and encouraging it to become democratic. As a part of the last process, it was decided to declare a moratorium on new investment in Germany until reconstruction had proceeded far enough to enable fair valuations to be established. In particular, while foreign investment might have stimulated recovery, it seemed undesirable to enable individuals or businesses abroad to acquire German interests when there was doubt that the sale was voluntary, at least so long as there was some question as to which plants might be removed for reparations, and while monetary conditions were chaotic. German interests might find themselves selling real long-run values for marks acquired through black-market operations in cigarettes and candy bars. And Germans might be willing to sell a majority share to foreigners to escape reparations removals, since the policy was to use foreign-owned property for reparation deliveries only if no German-owned plant were available. The basic theme, however, was that a Germany which had sold out its industrial assets at fire-sale prices would not be ready for democratization. Restitution of Jewish property to owners then abroad and priority to German- over foreign-owned property in reparations removals of plant and equipment would substantially raise the proportion of foreign-owned total industrial property from its low prewar percentage. To permit American, and British and French, industrialists to pick up potentially profitable enterprises cheaply would run counter to the national purposes for which the war had been fought. The policy was one which recommended itself to the top economic officials in the Department of State and in Germany. It also appealed to Secretary of State James F. Byrnes, Undersecretary William L. Clayton, and General Lucius D. Clay, all of whom were Southern by birth, or quickly did so when it was explained to them that the foreign and American interests hovering over the wreckage of the German economy were "carpetbaggers."

It is of some interest that all requests to the Department of State by American firms were predicated on making profits indirectly rather than immediately; this tends to support the theory of direct investment advanced in the last lecture. A large manufacturing company whose plant in the Eastern Zone had been seized by the Russians sought an opportunity to buy the plant of its largest rival as a means of maintaining its "market position." An oil company that had never operated in Germany because of the "As Is" agreement of 1928 (which declared that oil-company marketing would remain "as is") sought to buy out a German firm that had been engaged in selling synthetic gasoline produced by coal-tar products—an activity that was then prohibited to the defeated country—as a means of getting a distribution network to enable it to refine crude oil and sell the products. The fundamental interest was to obtain an outlet for crude oil. Refining and marketing products have not been profitable in Germany since the war, but selling crude to Germany from the Middle East has been.[1] A nonferrous metals company, under an antitrust court judg-

1. For an account of the difficulties of companies engaged solely in refining and distribution, see "Anti-U.S. Outcry Fills Meeting of Stockholders in Swiss Town," *New York Times* (May 21, 1966). The dispatch described the indignation of stockholders called upon to ratify a decision by the Italo-Suisse Holding Company of Geneva, with a 60 percent interest in Raffineries du Rhône, to sell a refinery and other assets to a group of eight oil companies headed by the Standard Oil Company (New Jersey). The refinery, at Collombey in Switzerland, had been operating at a deficit ever since its construction in 1963.

ment to dissolve its 50-50 partnership with a German chemical company in a joint subsidiary in a third country, wanted to buy out the German interest rather than sell its own share in a disorganized market. A motion picture company, represented ironically by a lawyer who had a leading role in formulating the Morgenthau plan for the pastoralization of Germany, wanted to spend frozen Reichsmarks, accumulated by exhibiting motion pictures with no chance of conversion into dollars, for downtown theaters in major German cities, or so-called showcases. Here the monopolistic feature of vertical integration with limited outlets is evident.[2]

The moratorium on foreign investment was lifted after monetary reform and the restoration of German sovereignty. It is not clear that German interests would have been willing to sell substantial interests to foreigners under the chaotic conditions which prevailed up to 1948–50, but the incident is worth remembering as a balance to the view that United States policy is to impose economic colonialism on the world.

2. One remarkable incident occurred in February 1947 at a meeting of the Council of Foreign Ministers in Moscow. British Foreign Secretary Ernest Bevin put forward to the Secretary of State, George C. Marshall, at the request of a British company and furnished to the Foreign Secretary by a British government department, a petition that the United States reconsider a decision denying the right to an *American* firm to buy certain German assets. The basis of the request was that the British and American firms had worked together in the past, and the British firm thought that the Secretary of State might be induced to change his decision if an allied government saw no harm in granting the permission. When the decision to leave matters as they stood was communicated to Bevin, he was said to have been indignant that his first communication as a Labor Foreign Secretary to Secretary Marshall should have been to ask a favor for an international "cartel."

One further such episode may be worth recounting briefly. It will be remembered that the Potsdam Agreement provided, inter alia, that the Soviet Union would receive German assets in its zone of occupation in Austria as reparations. To test whether the Soviet Union regarded such assets as normal foreign-owned property, subject to the laws of the sovereign power—in this case Austria—or whether it claimed extraterritoriality, the United States suggested to Austria that it undertake to nationalize with compensation the entire oil production industry in Austria, including both American assets and Soviet recently acquired and previously German properties. Happily for those who would have had the task of explaining to the American public that the government was recommending the nationalization of its citizens' property abroad, the Soviet Union denied that the Austrian government had the right to nationalize the assets acquired by the U.S.S.R. as reparations or to dictate their use, insisting in fact on the sort of extraterritoriality it typically accuses capitalistic countries of effecting. As a result, all nationalization action was given up. It may be observed that in due course, the Soviet Union did abandon its claim to these properties in eastern Austria in exchange for funded payments. On this occasion, American properties were not nationalized.

The issues today largely turn on a legal question: What right has the United States to try to make the subsidiaries of its national corporations conform in their foreign actions to the overall foreign policy of the United States? The United States has an interest in assisting its citizens to prosper. To this end it renders them general support in their foreign operations. It is also committed to international amity and to uphold the sovereignty of foreign countries in their own jurisdiction. At the same time, when its policies differ from those abroad, from time to time it will seek to use the foreign subsidiaries of United States corporations as a means of effecting that foreign policy.

Take, for example, United States policy on trading with the Soviet and Chinese blocs, which is much more restrictive than the policies of its allies and friends, including especially Canada and Britain. To the extent that the United States explicitly or implicitly requires foreign subsidiaries of United States firms to conform to United States foreign policy rather than the foreign policy of the countries where they are located, it impinges on foreign sovereignty. Or if the French government wants I.B.M. France to sell it a particular type of computer needed to make progress with the production of its nuclear bomb and the United States, committed to preventing the spread of nuclear weapons, urges against it, the French concern, which is owned by an American, becomes caught up in international politics in a complex way.

Economists have no business dealing with these legal subtleties beyond pointing out their existence. I learned early in this field that there is no ultimate legal truth. United States jurisprudence pierces the corporate veil (the mere fact that the subsidiary is incorporated in a foreign jurisdiction and is a juridical person of foreign citizenship) and focuses on the fact of ownership—except where United States interests are served by not piercing. British law, on the other hand, places emphasis on the nationality of the subsidiary incorporation—except where it is particularly beneficial to pierce the corporate veil. But while these are matters to be settled by lawyers— along with much else in the field of international investment—the economist cannot hope to dwell in ignorance of the existence of conflicts of jurisdictions which arise in such narrowly economic questions as taxation and balances of payments, as well as in foreign policy more generally.

A lawyer who takes his own case has a fool for a client. It is even more foolish for an economist to make pronouncements in legal matters. Nonetheless, the weight of legal opinion, so far as I can observe it, is against the United States practice of conducting its foreign security, military, and even economic policy through its corporate nationals, when they are organized abroad under foreign laws. It would be legitimate, under this view, for the Department of State to prevent I.B.M. New York from selling a computer to the French Force de Frappe, but not I.B.M. France. If I.B.M. France does not manufacture the particular model, it cannot be said to be under any French requirement to get one from New York, if the New York head office is not allowed to furnish it. But where I.B.M. Paris could furnish one, and the Department of State asks I.B.M. New York not to let it do so, the company is clearly in a cleft stick. It is damned in the United States if it does and in France if it does not.

This lecture, I fear, begins to tend to the anecdotal, but an Australian incident may be apposite. During World War II, the Australian government wanted to undertake the production of aircraft in Australia and naturally turned for assistance to the General Motors-Holden company, among others. L. J. Harnett, the general manager, was aware that General Motors in Detroit had had an unhappy experience with its investment in the Douglas Aircraft Company, and had a rule of not investing further in aircraft. In consequence he did not ask for head office permission but merely went ahead and cooperated in the aircraft venture.[3] In the political and military sphere, local policy may differ not only with the national policies of the investing company, but with rules of thumb developed by the investor.

The clash of foreign policies within the confines of the international corporation will be discussed further at the end of this lecture, and again in the last lecture. It is the essence of the political difficulty over direct investment, and there is no escape from it.

Taxation[4]

United States policy after the war was to encourage foreign investment. It was recognized that the International Bank for Reconstruction and Development could not provide all the capital needed for economic development abroad. There was little prospect, it was felt, that the foreign bond market in New York would revive. Loans and grants for development were provided unilaterally through various agencies—the Economic Cooperation Administration, Mutual Security Agency, and Agency for International Development—and to a lesser degree multilaterally through the United Nations. The hope for reducing the amount of foreign aid, it was thought, particularly during the Eisenhower administration, was to rely on private investment in the less developed countries.

3. L. J. Harnett, *Big Wheels and Little Wheels* (Melbourne, Lansdowne Press, 1964), Chap. 15.

4. This discussion and that of the next section have benefited particularly from Krause and Dam, *Federal Tax Treatment of Foreign Income*, especially Chap. 4.

Early stimuli to private investment were the tax credit under which foreign income taxes paid would be credited on income taxes due on dividends remitted to the United States; the Western Hemisphere Trade Corporation, which gave an investment credit of 14 percentage points on investments made in the Western Hemisphere that qualified by meeting certain rigorous standards, largely earning the vast majority of its income in active trade or business outside the United States; and tax deferral. The tax credit was designed to provide tax neutrality for American investors between foreign and domestic investments by preventing double taxation of corporate income. It inevitably had other and unanticipated effects, such as encouraging foreign countries to raise the level of their corporate income taxation to United States rates, which would increase their revenue at the expense of the United States government without hurting the foreign corporation (except for the deferral feature). It also led certain oil-producing countries to convert royalty arrangements to income taxes so as to raise income for the corporation by increasing the amount it could deduct from payment of United States taxes without lowering the country's own receipts. To the extent that the tax credit has led to increased receipts for foreign countries or for United States corporations operating abroad on inframarginal investments, without stimulating new investment, it has constituted foreign aid or added corporate rents at the American taxpayers' expense.

Tax deferral arises from the fact that United States corporate taxation is levied on dividends remitted to the United States rather than on income earned. Where corporate tax rates abroad were lower than those in the United States—52 percent up to the income tax reduction of 1964 and 48 percent thereafter—companies would defer taxes by reinvesting profits. Since such deferral was not available on domestic investments, it constituted a departure from tax neutrality, and in effect constituted an interest-free loan from the government to the corporation of the taxes eventually due. Where profit remittance was deferred until the corporation was liquidated, the ultimate tax liability could be halved by treating accumulated profits as a capital gain rather than as dividends. In particular cases, holding companies were established in low-tax jurisdictions to receive profits from one or more countries and reinvest them or hold them in liquid form. Where a particular form of income was not taxed in one jurisdiction, e.g. royalty payments in France, it could be paid into such a holding company and escape all taxation until ultimately remitted. In some instances, merchandise was shipped from the United States, or from one production center abroad to an export market, at stated prices which represented little or no profit, and invoices were marked up in the tax-haven office to earn profits there with minimal tax.

During the 1950s a variety of devices for further stimulating foreign investment was explored, but no satisfactory one of widespread usefulness was found. By 1961, when concern was felt for the balance of payments of the United States, however, the Treasury thought it desirable to move toward tax neutrality, especially on investments in Europe, by eliminating tax deferrals and imposing United States income taxes, to the extent not offset by the foreign tax credit, on income earned abroad rather than dividends remitted. Some of the arguments relating to the balance of payments will be examined presently. But a storm of indignation at the proposed change of rules arose from the business community, and in the end, though the Treasury was able to restrict the use of tax-havens through limiting deferrals to operating corporations, it was obliged to yield on tax deferral generally. The Revenue Act of 1962 tightened up the regulations in a number of ways, such as making all ultimate repatriation subject to corporate income tax regardless of whether the overseas operation is being liquidated or not, but tax deferral stands.

The United States government does oppose tax-sparing agreements, which have been sought by a number of countries. Where a country wants to stimulate United States investment by offering tax concessions, present United States tax-credit provisions mean that the reduced tax abroad is offset by a higher tax in the United States. A tax-sparing agreement would provide that any concession given by a host country to a company would accrue to the investing company and not merely enlarge the tax received by the investor's country. In the short run, while the balance of payments is regarded as in deficit, tax sparing which stimulates outflows from the United States can be regarded as contrary to the United States interest. Over the longer run, the agreements present the danger that the less developed countries may competitively erode their tax structures in seeking to entice foreign investors, as some states and localities within the United States have done. This paternalistic view of the interests of the developing countries, which they may not appreciate fully, is the basis for the United States government's failure to ask Congress to ratify the tax-sparing agreement with Israel, or to enter into further such agreements with other countries.

Since the Revenue Act of 1962, Assistant Secretary of the Treasury Stanley S. Surrey has stated that the Department might take a closer look at transfer pricing in transactions between firm and subsidiary or among subsidiaries in an effort to see that international corporations do not divert taxable profits abroad from United States taxation, which is applicable only in those countries where the rate of corporate income tax is lower than the 48 percent charged in the United States. Except to the extent that there are larger depreciation and other allowances abroad than in the United States, however, there is no reason to expect arbitrary pricing of intercompany transactions to divert income from the United States rather than the other way. Indeed, insofar as there may be a greater risk on foreign than on domestic investment, American services such as rents and royalties on patents, industrial technology and management service fees, are more likely to be overpriced than underpriced. But tax collectors in all countries must remain alert.

A particular problem is presented by oil. As already indicated, oil companies and host countries initially arranged that oil royalties were converted to income taxes which were accorded a credit in payment of United States taxes, thus in effect transferring tax revenue from the United States to oil-producing countries without affecting the companies. More recently, after the spreading practice of giving substantial discounts on oil below the posted price for most customers, the countries have calculated income taxes due from the companies on profits calculated on posted prices, rather than on actual profits based on actual prices. If it were interested in maximizing its tax revenue, the United States could now argue that an income tax on a notional price is not really an income tax at all but rather an excise tax, and as such is not entitled to qualify for the foreign income tax credit under United States legislation. But such an interpretation would be regarded as a hostile act against business and foreign investment.

Balance of Payments

The impact of direct investment on the balance of payments of the United States is a subject that is thoroughly
confused. The confusion is compounded of many elements. In essence, it rests on the inability of the parties
to the dispute to agree on a single analytical model that
relates direct investment to the balance of payments.
That such agreement is not forthcoming is no surprise.
There is no single analytical model on which agreement
is possible.

We will come presently to the choice among one-shot
investment models, continuing investment at a constant
rate, continuous investment at a constantly growing level,
and investment that is needed today to sustain past investment on a fruitful basis. First, however, let me illustrate the problem by dealing with the decisions faced by
the Office of Foreign Direct Investment established in
the Department of Commerce to operate the mandatory
restrictions on direct investment of January 2, 1968.

The United States wants direct investment, but it does
not want its adverse balance-of-payments effect. It recognizes that after a time, when dividends and interest plus
induced exports begin to flow, direct investment helps
the balance of payments. But in the short run, it hurts, or
it may hurt. The Office of Foreign Direct Investment has
therefore been enjoined to permit investment but to
limit its adverse balance-of-payments effect. Requests for
permission to make investments will be judged in terms
of balance-of-payments effects.

This broad statement of principles is understandable,
but it rests on faulty analysis. There is no way of judging
the balance-of-payments effect of a single transaction
without knowing what would happen if it did not occur,

and the complete chain of consequences if it does occur. Both are unknowable. In economic jargon, decisions are made on the basis of partial-equilibrium analysis, with *ceteris paribus,* when they require general-equilibrium analysis, or *mutatis mutandis.*

Examples may clarify the issue. The Office of Foreign Direct Investment must decide whether to allow acquisitions made with capital equipment, patents, technology, exchanges of shares, and so forth. On a partial-equilibrium basis, with other things equal, there is no adverse balance-of-payments effect, but only, after time has elapsed to enable the project to pay out, a favorable one. But this analysis is inadequate. Would the capital equipment have been sold anyhow? If so, the decline in exports that earn foreign exchange adversely affects the balance of payments. Or what about a foreign investment financed abroad? The government recognizes that when the source of financing is dividends that would otherwise be remitted there is a balance-of-payments hurt as much as there would be if capital funds were brought from home. But suppose General Motors finances its Antwerp plant entirely in Europe by borrowing the $100 million in Belgium. Pressure on capital markets raises Belgian and European interest rates. At the margin, Europeans with United States securities will be encouraged to sell them and bring back the proceeds to lend in Europe. One can close the flow of capital through bonds, bank loans, direct investment, Canadian insurance companies, and so forth, but so long as one or more conduits are left open, such as the right of foreign holders of United States securities—amounting to $14 billion—to withdraw their capital, direct investment may still lead to capital outflow.

The impossibility of knowing what the general-equilibrium consequences of any particular action in foreign investment will be puts the government in an awkward position. We approve of regulations by laws, not men. Since it is possible to explore part of the way beyond the partial-equilibrium position, two identical requests may elicit different responses from the authorities. Company A will be allowed to transfer capital abroad to pay off a bank loan or to make good on a guarantee of a loan by its subsidiary; Company B, which equally wants to pay down its indebtedness, is refused permission because it admits that the foreign bank will renew the loan. Investment is permitted through an exchange of stock with a foreign firm or through purchase of the assets owned abroad by another United States firm, on the ground that there is no balance-of-payments impact; but in the first case, the foreign investor can turn around and sell the United States securities, remitting home the proceeds, and in the second, it might have been possible with effort to sell the foreign assets to a foreigner.

On a more general rather than case-by-case level, the problem in deciding the impact of direct investment on the balance of payments is that of choosing the appropriate model. There is little difficulty in agreeing about the several effects on the balance of payments, pro and con, or more properly credit and debit. These are set out in a National Industrial Conference Board study and come out to ten, five of which affect receipts: repatriated earnings, related exports of capital equipment, related exports of raw materials, exports of types of goods other than those produced abroad, which are more readily sold now that the company has a "foreign presence," and royalties and fees for patents, industrial knowledge, and management services. The five debit items are the original capital outflow in a new investment, subsequent capital outflows to maintain existing investments, displaced merchandise exports, United States exports in third markets displaced by overseas production, and increased imports from new production abroad.[5]

How these various factors should be combined to estimate the effect of direct investment on the balance of payments is an open question, and so especially is the question of what sort of direct investment should be hypothesized. The Brookings Institution study, using coefficients derived from balance-of-payments statistics, assumed that for a given direct investment the impetus to new exports on capital equipment, raw materials, and other lines stimulated by the foreign presence would be 10.6 percent a year of the cumulated value of the investment. No allowance was made for the fact that capital-equipment exports are related to investment but not to output. Royalties and fees were estimated at 2.3 percent. Overall earnings were put at 16.8 percent a year, of which a little more than half (51.8 percent), or 8.7 percent of the cumulated investment, is repatriated (and 8.1 percent reinvested).[6] The import stimulus is put at 6.5 percent of the total investment though it is acknowledged that this may be unduly high, as applied to manufacturing investment in Europe, because of the spurt in automobile imports in the base years. There is no allowance for loss of exports because of the difficulties in estimations.

But the big question on which the Treasury expert and the spokesman for business divided sharply in the hearings on the Revenue Act of 1962 was whether one

5. Polk, Meister, and Veit, *U.S. Production Abroad*, p. 126.

6. The Brookings study makes a slip in stating that 8.7 percent is retained (Krause and Dam, pp. 72, 75, 76: Table notes, col. 5). The calculations correctly show 8.1 percent reinvested.

should assume a single investment or a shift in the investment schedule which meant a new level of investment repeated year after year.[7] On the Brookings figures, a single investment would worsen the balance of payments for a period of five to six years, and thereafter improve it as repatriated earnings and increased exports outweigh increased imports and the original investment has been successfully transferred. A continuous stream of investment, however, left the balance of payments in deficit for ten years before the cumulative negative effect was reversed. Indeed, the Brookings study adds another possibility, that instead of a steady stream there is a mounting one. It seems reckless to extrapolate for twenty years the 22 percent annual rate of increase in direct investment which occurred between 1956 and 1961. Exponential growth is highly sensitive over time to small changes in initial coefficients, and the annual rates of increase starting from an initial $1,000 reach absurd levels of new investment of $36,000, $44,000, and $53,000 in the eighteenth, nineteenth, and twentieth years. The Brookings conference on taxation of foreign income thought that a model somewhere between the constant stream and the increasing stream was the appropriate one, in contrast to the business community which regarded the single investment as the only possible model to consider.

But there are two major factors that the models do

7. See Philip W. Bell, "Private Capital Movements and the Balance of Payments Position," in U.S. Congress, Subcommittee on International Exchange and Payments of the Joint Economic Committee, *Factors Affecting the United States Balance of Payments,* 87th Congress, 2d Sess. (Washington, D.C., G.P.O., 1962), pp. 395–481, and the testimony of E. G. Collado, U.S. Congress, Senate Committee on Finance, *Hearings on H.R. 10650, Revenue Act of 1962,* 87th Congress, 2d Sess. (Washington, D.C., G.P.O., 1962), pp. 3232–46.

not consider, one positive, one negative. On the negative side, it will be remembered from the first lecture, new investment does not produce an immediate return, but pays off only over time. This means first that there is no flow of dividends to support the balance of payments beginning with year 2, and second that the further investment required after the first year, but before the rate of return has risen to its long-term level with no profits to reinvest, must come from the United States. The longer the delay in profitability the higher the total investment and the worse the balance of payments over time. On the positive side, however, is the contention of Professor Behrman that the models fail to take account of the fact that United States investment is largely financed abroad. Using 40 percent United States and 60 percent foreign financing, and 8 percent of the former transferred in kind, he has only 32 percent of the total sum as a debit in the balance of payments in the first year. On this showing, incremental exports of 12.5 percent plus 2.4 percent in remitted earnings to the United States per annum take care of the original balance of payments debit in little more than two years.[8] There is some doubt whether it is appropriate to apply coefficients based on balance-of-payments experience to a model that starts out from a different premise: the Brookings coefficients relate to the investment made from the United States, not to the total including foreign financing. But assuming this doubt is overcome in Professor Behrman's favor, his major positive effect, which consists in reducing the initial investment by 60 percent, may be largely offset by the delay in receipt of earnings which he and the others ignore.

8. Jack N. Behrman, "Foreign Investment Muddle: The Perils of Ad Hoccery," *Columbia Journal of World Business, 1* (Fall 1965).

How can this confusion be resolved? The National Industrial Conference Board attempts to do so by making a distinction between the "incremental" and the "organic" approaches. The incremental approach looks at a single overseas investment, profitable in itself, and traces its balance-of-payments effect through time. The Board rejects this way of looking at foreign investment. In its view, direct investment is organic. It relates to markets and competitive positions in markets, not to the calculation of profits on particular investment decisions. A given investment has no pay-out except in connection with a host of related previous and subsequent investments. To halt the flow of overseas investment would be to jeopardize the position of United States investors in foreign markets and threaten loss of income on past investments. On this showing there is no standing still: to stop is to lose but to go forward is to gain.

There is something to this view, certainly, but surely not everything. Where new investments have been undertaken and not yet come to fruition, it is sensible to continue them to completion and profitable operation. Additionally, it may be necessary to keep up with the growth of the market where it is expanding rapidly. During the 1950s when national income in many European countries was growing at 7 to 10 percent a year, and output in some markets like oil at close to 15 percent, it was important to expand at least at the same rate as the market and the industry. But the change in the character of European growth since that continent ran out of labor in the early 1960s has reduced overall rates of growth to more normal long-run levels of 3 and 4 percent a year. These make it possible for many companies to keep up with the market without new investment from the United States while remitting a substantial share of profit as dividends. And it must be recognized that much United States investment of recent years is based on faddism rather than sure profit prospects. New firms are undertaking foreign investment for the first time, with nothing organic about their operations. The incremental analysis applies to many of these, and in its negative formulation, with long delays in profitability and limited, if any, offsets from foreign financing.

The fact is that direct investment by the United States, especially in European manufacturing, was in grave danger of being overdone when the mandatory restrictions of January 1, 1968 were imposed. Investors have a well-known propensity for following the leader—too far—as exemplified throughout history in the tulip mania, the South Sea Bubble, the 1925 Florida land boom, or the 1929 stock market. Profits have been lower in Europe over the past five years, as costs have risen faster than prices. The level of stock prices has declined. In the field of portfolio investment in European equities, the bubble expanded in the early 1960s, and burst. There is currently very little Wall Street interest in European securities, apart from an occasional issue like K.L.M. But the direct investment boom kept on.

Part of recorded direct investment, to be sure, does not consist in plant and equipment, but in accumulated dividends or open-book credits which subsidiaries of American companies have left in liquid form in the Euro-dollar market. The Department of Commerce accounting method scores this as direct investment when it is in fact highly liquid cash, usually held in dollars. Moreover, the prospect of restrictions on direct investment in 1964 and 1965, and again after the devaluation of sterling in November 1967, led many firms to prepare by accumulating funds, or borrowing in Europe in advance of requirements.[9] If restrictions on foreign investment were to be relaxed, foreign investment might well decline rather than expand.

On the whole, it seems sufficient to emphasize the "demonstration-effect" character of much American direct investment (and Secretary of the Treasury Henry H. Fowler did in his speech at Grotonville in the spring of 1966), to warn some of the smaller firms that it is the suckers who come into an investment movement at the end and are left holding the bag, and to rely on market forces to shake down direct investment to an appropriate level. Voluntary restrictions, in which private interests are expected to serve public purposes rather than their own end of making profits, are a poor way to run the system. Mandatory restrictions on a case-by-case method may be worse.

The mandatory restrictions on direct investment are the latest (as this is written) in a series of efforts to improve the balance of payments. Outside of direct investment there have been tying of foreign aid,[10] diversion of government purchases from foreign to domestic suppliers, the interest equalization tax, the Gore amendment extending the tax on bonds to bank loans, and most recently the request for taxes on tourist expenditure.

9. See Lydecker, "Direct Foreign Investment and the Balance of Payments," pp. 60, 98.

10. Note that this too always improves the balance of payments on a partial-equilibrium basis, with other things equal, but may not do so if aid recipients change other things, and, specifically, shift normal imports which would otherwise have been paid for by dollar-earning exports to an aid basis, diverting the dollars thus released to other purposes, including additions to resources and purchases from other countries.

In direct investment, the Voluntary Credit Restraint Program applied originally in February 1965 to 400 firms. In November of the same year another 500 firms were added. In the initial phase, the emphasis was on restricting the export of capital from the United States. Gradually this extended to improving the impact of the corporation on the balance of payments, including increasing the return flow of dividends from abroad. The mandatory restrictions established three classes of countries—those developed countries with strong balances of payments (especially in the European Economic Community), others such as Britain and the Dominions with less strong balances, and the less developed countries, from which all but 35, 65, and 105 percent of 1965–66 (base year) profits were to be transferred home.

But the Mandatory Credit Restraint Program is an order by the United States directing the behavior of foreign corporations. In 1966, the Canadian government bridled at the idea that Canadian firms, even if subsidiaries of United States companies, would be told by a foreign power how to distribute earnings.[11] In January 1968, when Undersecretary of State Nicholas Katzenbach consulted the French government about the United States program, he was given an oblique warning, which was repeated by Premier Michel Debré in a press conference on January 24, 1968.[12] Beggar-thy-neighbor action

11. "Canada to Urge U.S. Affiliates to Ignore Johnson Guidelines," *New York Times* (March 11, 1966).
12. "French Endorse U.S. Dollar Policy," *New York Times* (January 7, 1968), and "Call to Repatriate Overseas Earnings Stirs Legal Snarls," *New York Times* (January 29, 1968). The French attitude as summarized by official sources included:
Subsidiaries of American companies in France are legally French companies with the same access to the financial market

can take place in a variety of international links which lead to stalemate: A taxes imports, for example, while B subsidizes them; or A taxes imports and B taxes the identical goods as exports, which rapidly dries up trade. Countries are well aware today of the dangers of beggar-thy-neighbor policies in the field of merchandise trade. It is not so obvious that they have thought through the implications of seeking to control the balance of payments in direct-investment items.

We return to balance-of-payments considerations in the next lecture in discussing the French contention that United States monetary policies have resulted in pressure to worsen the United States balance of payments and in particular to make it possible for United States companies to buy French firms with monies borrowed from France. There is much in the view that the United States "deficit" has been a monetary, not a spending or goods-price phenomenon. But this, as we shall see, does not mean easy acceptance of the French contention.

One final point on the balance of payments. It is of some interest to know whether United States direct in-

---

and Government credits as other French companies. If the United States imposes new regulations on them, "notably regarding the repatriation of profits . . ." it will be impossible not to draw the consequences.

The consequences implied in this account are presumably the cutting off of U.S. subsidiaries from access to French sources of credit. In an Associated Press dispatch of January 16, 1968, however ("U.S. Action May Force France to Shell Out Gold," *Atlanta Constitution* [January 17, 1968]), it is stated:

Experts say France has weapons to stop a hemorrhage of its reserves if French officials feel they are made to carry an unfair and disproportionate part of the load. One step, a severe one, could be currency restriction to block repatriation of U.S. companies' earnings. No one expects it to come to that.

vestment conforms to a demand or to a supply model in terms of United States business conditions; does it, that is, respond positively or negatively to an upswing in domestic prosperity? In a demand model, a given supply of corporate cash flow—corporate profits and depreciation and depletion allowances—is allocated between domestic and overseas uses depending on relative profitability. When business expansion in the United States exceeds that in Europe, as it has since 1964, one would expect overseas investment to slow down and United States investment to pick up. There were signs in 1966 that investment demands inside the United States were so imperious that overseas commitments were being cut back.

In a supply model, on the other hand, there is a fixed profit margin in favor of overseas investment—during a long transitional period in which firms change their horizons from the domestic to the international scene—and how much is invested abroad depends upon the size of the cash flow and especially the variable portion, profits. When profits rise, direct investment increases; when they fall, it subsides for lack of funds. There is no presumption that one or another model will predominate throughout the breadth of American industry, of course, and it is difficult to sort out the question empirically because of such interference as "demonstration effect." The organic view would deny both relations, insisting that investment grows in both markets at the rates at which the markets expand, and that finance through profits is not controlling. But a graduate student at M.I.T., Dwight Jaffee, has shown econometrically that there is a strong presumption based on the recent evidence covering 1952–65 to favor the supply view. It is by no means certain that this model would apply at any and all times, since one would expect it to obtain primarily in intermediate and transitional stages. My own deductive view would be that the supply model has applied during the particular period of the 1950s and early 1960s when American firms were extending their horizon from the national to the international scene, but that once the pell-mell stampede to invest abroad is brought to a halt—perhaps by relaxing the restrictions—the model will switch, except in new industries, to a demand one. But my faith in this conclusion is limited.

Antitrust Policy

One widely held view in the United States is that firms expand through horizontal integration abroad because they are forbidden by our antitrust laws to do so at home. By widening their control of the market to become worldwide, they obtain more control of price. Acquisition of a foreign firm prevents it from exporting to the United States, and is to this extent in "restraint of trade."

As indicated in the first lecture, this pattern is possible but it is by no means necessary. In competitive industries it may still be desirable to undertake direct investment, to coordinate company operations at successive stages of production more efficiently than atomistic markets can do. An investor with a big advantage over his foreign competition in a market protected by tariffs or by its bulk-gaining character, which attracts production to locations near the market, can increase competition abroad without affecting it at home. It is even possible that direct investment abroad can increase competition at home and abroad at the same time.

The best example of this last statement, to which brief allusion has already been made, is the acquisition by

General Electric of most of Machines Bull in computers and of parts of Olivetti, and by Radio Corporation of America of parts of Siemens. In the computer field, the International Business Machines Company was far in the lead in the United States and in Europe, with a sprinkling of smaller American companies—Sperry Rand, Burroughs and so forth—and one British company, International Computers and Tabulators, well in the rear. General Electric had fallen behind through lack of central attention to the computer and automation developments at a time when its decentralized structure concentrated responsibility in separate product divisions, unconcerned with new areas of company activity. Similarly, on its side of the ocean Machines Bull had made a brilliant, independent entry into computers at the mechanical, card-sorting level, but was finding difficulty and losing money in effecting a transition to electronic techniques. In union there is strength; united we stand, divided we fall; and similar slogans. There was nothing more natural than that these new entrants into the ring should combine. Where economies of scale exist, it is difficult to start small. International mergers or acquisitions may be a means of increasing competition rather than reducing it.

But not all direct investment increases competition. There is the extension of horizontal monopoly, as mentioned above. It is particularly significant, perhaps, that in some areas like banking, somewhat archaic United States laws, a residue of the Populist movement, forbid commercial banks to organize branches outside a county but have no provision to prevent their spreading all over the rest of the world.

Again, the Department of Justice in the United States is worried that when companies cooperate in a foreign venture, they may get into habits of understanding which will spill over to the United States and result in market sharing, price maintenance, repression of new products, and the like. The Arabian American Oil Company (Aramco) has four owners. Originally the Standard Oil Company of California, which discovered the oil, sold half its interest to the Texas Oil Company in order to obtain a marketing organization. As the size of the find grew it was necessary to obtain more capital and the Standard Oil Company of New Jersey and the Socony Mobil Oil Company (now the Mobil Oil Corporation) bought in to provide the needed funds. But while these firms collaborate in Saudi Arabia, they are competitors in other markets, including the United States. And a similar situation exists in the South Andes Copper Company in Peru, a venture whose capital demands were too large for any one of the American copper companies but which Anaconda, Kennecott, Cerro de Pasco, and the others undertook together without, presumably, affecting their arm's-length competition elsewhere in the rest of the world. These foreign operations have each been approved by the Department of Justice as unrelated to competition in the United States, but to keep attitudes and habits of work distinct in different marketing areas seems to the outsider quite a trick. On the other side of the argument, however, it is of some interest to note that the Standard Oil Company of California and the Texas Oil Company decided in 1967 to divide their European marketing organization and to go their separate competitive ways instead of their former joint collaborative way. Interests do then seem to differ in one area even when they are joined in others.

Or competition in the United States can be decreased by direct investment abroad in a more subtle way. In a concentrated industry with foreign competitors in the American market, an investment by a leading firm in the home market of its foreign rivals in the United States market conveys an implicit instruction not to rock the boat. This is the case of mutual invasion of each other's markets mentioned in the first lecture. There is little that the United States can do about conspiracy abroad to restrict sales to the United States market, especially if it is not really conspiracy, but approaches more nearly "conscious parallel action," or silent threat and equally silent receiving and acting on the message. It cannot claim jurisdiction over what happens abroad between foreign corporations, and the view that it can pierce the veil of American ownership of a subsidiary formed under foreign laws is not universally held. What is called for, a subject reserved mainly for the last lecture, is harmonization of antitrust policies, or an international agreement on principles, with some national or international mechanism to apply them on a case-by-case basis. The Swedish and European Economic Community device of requiring registration of all business agreements is helpful but by no means solves the issue, unless it is followed up by dealing with unwritten understandings on one hand and an agreement on principles on the other. In particular, the separate countries must develop mutual policies that abhor restraint of trade within and without, and must not limit the eradication of restraint practices to those affecting the home market. In Europe, it is unhappy that the Coal and Steel Community Court of Justice ruled that the High Authority had no right to forbid price discrimination against outsiders, even though it was required to prevent it at home. In the United States, the Sherman and Clayton Anti-Trust Acts are paralleled by the Webb-Pomerene Act which permits, or encourages, agreements among rival producers in this country for the purpose of selling abroad.

But most important, I think, is that any agreement on principles must be applied on a case-by-case basis, since there is no rule of thumb as to whether any given direct investment will improve or reduce competition, worldwide, without some knowledge of the particular facts. If Alcan buys out the Aardal og Sunndal Verk, world competition in aluminum is decreased, whereas if Reynolds or Kaiser had bought the same company, the same would not hold. The true believer who suspects that all direct investment is subversive to competition is wrong.[13]

Apart from its effects on foreign policy generally and on taxation, on the balance of payments and on antitrust development, and in the absence of other external diseconomies, it may be assumed that direct investment benefits the United States and the rest of the world. The Brookings Institution makes a distinction between the pretax income and the after-tax. The United States gains from foreign direct investment up to the point where the after-tax profit rate on foreign investment is equal to the pretax rate of return on domestic investment, whereas from a world point of view such investment should be pushed to the point where the pretax rate of return abroad is equal to the pretax rate in the United States.[14] But this is a short-run view in which the United States acts as a monopolist. In the long run, a country must not be so greedy. Foreign investment benefits the

13. For a discussion of this subject, see U.S. Congress, *International Aspects of Antitrust, Hearings* Before the Senate Subcommittee on Antitrust and Monopoly of the Committee on the Judiciary, 89th Congress, 2d Sess., pursuant to Senate Resolution 191, parts 1 and 2.

14. Krause and Dam, p. 59.

United States and the world when it earns higher returns abroad than at home (provided monopoly is reduced rather than increased) with the taxes collected by the country that provides governmental services. In the short run, the added cost of such services to a country approaches zero. For more substantial amounts of investment, this may not be the case. The cosmopolitan and long-run view of the matter requires comparison between pretax rates of return in the two countries, or post-tax, but not the pretax rate in one country with the post-tax rate in the other.[15]

The Interests of Labor and Capital

But while the United States as a whole may benefit from the substantial outflow of capital which would equalize rates of return at home and abroad (after discount for real risk), it is clear that not every interest in the United States would benefit equally. In particular the return to capital would rise, as there would be relatively less of it, and returns to labor and land would decline, since they would be employed with less capital each. This is a static view, to be sure, and dynamic considerations of higher rates of growth with or without foreign investment, under the appropriate assumptions, might change the results. There is in economics a Stolper-Samuelson theorem which discusses the effects of trade on goods prices and through them on factor prices and factor in-

15. For a useful discussion of the "optimum rate of foreign investment" which reviews the work of D. MacDougall, M. C. Kemp, and R. W. Jones and concurs that agreements to avoid double taxation are Pareto-optimal by means of avoiding optimum taxes followed by retaliation, see Koichi Hamada, "Strategic Aspects of Taxation in Foreign Investment Income," *Quarterly Journal of Economics, 80,* No. 3 (August 1966), 361–75.

come distribution. When factors move directly, the returns to the factors that remain behind or are at hand to receive an immigrant factor supply are more directly affected.

The case is particularly dramatic where capital moves abroad to produce for the market at home. The Mesabi range was converted from a rich part of the country to a poor one by the exhaustion of its rich iron ores and the turning abroad by the steel companies to new iron mines in Quebec, Venezuela, Liberia, and so on. Texas oil interests are not partial to Saudi Arabia, Kuwait, Venezuela, Libya. Hollywood labor tries to draw a fine line of distinction between motion pictures that are made abroad because of their local color or, some years ago, to use up blocked exchange, and those that seek cheaper labor. Labor unions went on opposing the importation of watch movements after some of the leading domestic companies, such as Hamilton, decided that they should join them, since they couldn't lick them, and constructed plants in Switzerland and Japan.

In the middle years of the union movement in the United States, before and after World War I, there developed runaway industries, particularly in clothing, which moved from New York to Rochester, Chicago, Baltimore, Richmond, and beyond in an effort to escape the higher wages demanded by effective unionism. The labor movement answer to runaway plants has been national unions. The CIO, and later the AFL-CIO, drive to organize the South has cynically been characterized as motivated less by an interest in unionism for southern workers than the desire to protect northern industry by raising wages in the South.

The international concerns of the AFL-CIO have also been partly humanitarian and partly based on self-interest: to raise wages abroad and slow down potential imports. But the movement of United States capital abroad for production for the domestic market is comparatively new. Thus there has been little indication that the entrepreneurs are regarded as runaways or that American unions will organize internationally to move toward equalization of wages through collective bargaining rather than bidding up foreign wages and reducing the demand for American labor. But it begins. Walter Reuther of the United Automobile Workers has plans to organize the automotive industry in fourteen countries. The long gap between the initial announcement in 1962 and the later planning stages in 1966 suggests that there are more important matters on the UAW agenda.[16]

Organized labor in a number of countries has opposed immigration (but not, interestingly enough, in others such as Switzerland and Germany). In the United States, the movement against immigration goes back to the craft unions whose early opposition, in the face of the tradition of the United States as an asylum for the persecuted and the poor of other countries, produced the Foran Act of 1885, outlawing contract labor.[17] The ostensible reason for restricting immigration, of course, is that it subjects foreign workers to intolerable conditions. But it is curious that organized labor has been so quiescent on the matter of direct investment.

Certainly business and financial interests have clamored for freedom of capital movement, opposing the attempt of the Treasury to move toward "tax neutrality"

16. See the statement of W. Reuther in *The New York Times* (May 6, 1962), and the reference in *The Economist* (June 18, 1966).

17. See Charlotte Erickson, *American Industry and the European Immigrant, 1860–1886* (Cambridge, Mass., Harvard University Press, 1957).

in the Revenue Act of 1962, the Voluntary Credit Restraint Program of February 1965, and the mandatory restrictions of 1968. Where the particular interest coincides with both the general interest and the tradition of laissez-faire, it is relatively easy to make an egocentric case in the guise of high-minded statesmanship. Labor may have been inhibited by the fact that its particular interest in lower capital costs through restrictions on its export, and in resultant higher wages through combining each unit of labor with more capital, has been contrary to the general interest. It seems unlikely, however. One must put the limited nature of the reaction of labor against capital exports down as something of a puzzle and in the future keep an eye on this possible source of support for those interests abroad which also oppose direct investment from the United States.

The United States as Neo-Imperialist

I conclude this lecture with a brief disquisition on the widespread view outside the United States, to some extent shared by "liberal" elements inside the country, that United States firms engaged in direct investment are weapons through which the United States asserts its power in the world. It will satisfy no one who entertains settled convictions on the issue. The foreign critic is persuaded that the United States government's objective is political power; the direct investor on the whole tends to believe that he is not supported abroad sufficiently to achieve his legitimate economic ends because of American government political timidity. Anyone like me who argues that governments are composed of intelligent individuals seeking to work out a course of action to achieve what is appropriate both for the individual firm and for the world economy in the face of conflicting interests, is at the most optimistic naïve, and probably a scoundrel, no matter which point of view is taken.

Should the United States government stay aloof altogether from direct investment questions? This demand is implicit in the Calvo doctrine, found in the constitutions of many Latin American countries, which states that a foreign investor's government may not interfere on his behalf in matters affecting his relationship with the host government.[18] It emerges as a suggestion by Edith T. Penrose in an article on "International Economic Relations and the Large International Firm."[19] But the United States government is far from so doing. It presses Japan for the liberalization of its rules on foreign investment as they adversely affect United States concerns;[20] it puts pressure on Mexico to sign an investment guarantee treaty at the behest of American companies with subsidiaries in that country;[21] it is "provoked" into protesting to Canada over legislation that restricts United States investment in a Canadian bank.[22] The days of sending gunboats and Marines to protect United States property abroad have gone, but it is widely maintained that the United States government works hand-in-glove with its business concerns, exerting diplomatic pressure

18. See M. von Whitman, *Government Risk-Sharing in Foreign Investment* (Princeton, N.J., Princeton University Press, 1965), pp. 46–47.

19. In Peter Lyon, ed., *New Orientations in International Relations* (London, Cass, 1968).

20. Joint communiqué of the U.S.-Japan Joint Economic Committee, *Department of State Bulletin, 57*, No. 1476 (October 9, 1967), p. 453, para. 4.

21. As alleged in Latin American newsletters.

22. "Canada Bank Battle," *New York Times* (February 1, 1967).

on their behalf and using them to extend United States power and interests.

The rejoinder to these allegations is evident. The United States enters into treaties of commerce, friendship, and navigation with friendly sovereign powers regarding the rights of its citizens to conduct business abroad and of nationals of foreign countries to conduct business in the United States. Through tax measures and investment guarantees it has promoted foreign investment in the interest of the economic recovery of foreign countries and, with respect to guarantees, only with their concurrence. Where a country like Japan closes itself off from the rest of the world, whether with tariffs, quota restrictions, nontrade barriers, or restrictions on investment, the United States, believing as it does in the widest possible freedom for commerce and capital movements, urges liberalization. There is nothing sinister in protests to foreign governments when they fail to live up to their international obligations, or in persuasion to extend the range of such mutual commitments. Like every government, the United States extends its protection to its citizens abroad, and seeks to promote their interests, within, to be sure, the laws laid down by the sovereign government.

There is something to be said for the view that the United States is so large and powerful, especially when it faces the less developed countries, that there ought to be a double standard of conduct. What is sauce for the goose should perhaps not be sauce for the goslings. Some are more equal than others. Many economists believe that the less developed countries might be given rights to discriminate in tariffs and export taxes against the developed countries, without evoking retaliation from the large and strong countries.

The left-wing point of view and the nationalist one maintain that the single liberal standard is nothing but a mask for exploitation, domination, and promulgation of the national culture.[23] But perhaps it is better to wait for a verdict on these charges until I have analyzed separate items in the bill of particulars drawn up by foreign countries against the international corporation.

23. A letter by Robin Mathews to the editor of *The Canadian Forum*, 47 (September 1967), p. 130, protesting my review of A. E. Safarian's *Foreign Ownership of Canadian Industry* (Toronto, McGraw-Hill Company of Canada, 1966), states:

> Economists must realize that so-called international corporations are patently not primarily concerned with efficiency except as efficiency is defined by a particular national culture in terms of particular national aspirations. Present so-called international corporations are intimately linked with the self-regarding policies of national and nationalist governments. Those facts [sic] are perhaps more true for the United States than for other countries operating companies on an international front.

United States Direct Investment in Europe and Japan

I now deal primarily with a list—a rather long list—of European and Japanese complaints against and objections to direct investment from the United States. But it should not be concluded from this recital that such investment is uniformly opposed. On the contrary, the European attitude is both varied and, in the countries that mainly oppose, ambivalent. Like the Japanese, moreover, it changes. The French Ambassador to the United States, Charles Lucet, said recently that the French attitude really remains the same. The answer to the question whether such investment could take place used to be "No, but." It is now unchanged, as "Yes, but."

This lecture lists the objections of Europeans to American direct investment, the problems created by American monsters, too big, too strong, with too much capital and too easy access to more to make competition fair, with un-European ways of doing business, escaping the control of the banking system in Germany and the capital controls used to police national plans in France, undermining European technological independence, distorting trade patterns, and adding to inflation—worst of all, frequently buying or building plants with money borrowed from the Europeans themselves. But before getting to these separate arguments, to be analyzed from the dubious point of view of an American economist, one must indicate that there is another side to the story. The Italians and the Belgians are almost entirely in favor of more American investment, and the Dutch used to be. British worries are limited. These countries, as well as much of the positive side of the French and German attitudes and the changing view of the Japanese, focus on the contribution that American industry makes to growth through new industries, new processes, competition for the obsolete, and high-level investment. In Belgium in particular it is felt that foreign investment goes into industries where the Belgians do not go—automobiles, electrical goods, electronics, petrochemicals, machinery, and so forth, representing the growth industries of the second half of the twentieth century in which Belgian entrepreneurship has been lamentably weak. And even in France when the country objected to a given industrial investment, the fact of the Common Market gave pause. In several significant industries, an initial exploration was made of an investment in France, which, after considerable delay in obtaining a decision from the French government, was transferred to Belgium. After several such episodes the French adopted the view that even in industries that are not wanted, if they are to be established anyhow in Europe, let it be in France. Thus one of the several turns in French policy toward foreign investment, amounting to three in five years.[1]

Too Big

Fortune magazine in the United States provides each year a list of the 500 largest corporations in the United States and the 200 largest outside, which provides a cata-

1. See Servan-Schreiber, *The American Challenge*, p. 18, where he identifies the policies as pro from 1959 to 1963, con until 1965, pro until 1966, when selective.

log for European complaints about United States direct investment. Whether by sales, assets, net profit, or employees, United States corporations are too big, though this claim is made without taking into consideration the optimistic American expression, "The bigger they come, the harder they fall." All sorts of comparisons are made, and more are possible. There were 80 United States companies with sales of more than $1 billion in 1966, and 21 European.[2] The largest European automobile plant, Volkswagenwerke, had 1966 sales of $2.5 billion, compared with $20.2 billion for General Motors, $12.2 billion for Ford, and $5.6 billion for Chrysler. While Royal Dutch Shell is second to the Standard Oil Company of New Jersey ($7.7 billion of sales to $12.2 billion), Imperial Chemical Industries second to DuPont ($2.4 billion of sales to $3.2 billion), and Unilever well ahead of Procter and Gamble ($5.3 billion of sales to $2.2 billion), in many industries there are two or three large American firms before the first European firm is reached.

This sort of comparison is of little moment. In the first place, the United States corporation does not have all its sales, assets, profits, or employees available for competing with European companies. Most of them are needed in the United States, or, in the case of the oil companies, in producing areas overseas. The resources that the companies can bring to bear against competitors in Europe are limited, and more nearly on the same order of magnitude as those of European companies. Second, and more important, size is by no means the dominant factor in competitive potential. Other things being equal, more resources are better than less, but other things are

2. For these and the following data, see *The Fortune Directory* (June 15, 1967), separately printed by *Fortune* (September 15, 1967).

seldom equal. Frequently, as stated, the bigger they come, the harder they fall. United States Steel Company was 4th in employees in 1966, 6th in assets, 8th in volume of sales, 14th in net profit, and 436th in percent of profits to invested capital. The 5 companies that come first in terms of profit on invested capital among the 500 top United States companies in sales are 190th, 173d, 194th, 300th, and 183d in terms of sales, while the 5 that come first in terms of sales are 45th, 237th, 284th, 152d, and 325th in rate of profit on invested capital. German economists, for example, recognize that size is by no means critical to success.[3] In markets, as in the prize ring, the good little man can beat the big average man, or at least survive in the ring with him. Size is an excellent talking point because the data are available. And where European companies are of less than optimum scale, whether as plants or firms, growth through expansion or mergers is possible and desirable, as the French, and lately the British, seem to be aware. But emphasis on size can be and is vastly overdone.

The reason it is overdone, of course, is that much European business is rendered unhappy by the thought of more, or more vigorous and energetic, competition. The French Confédération du Patronat Français is reported to have worked hard to restrict the entry of foreign enterprise into France, and into the European Economic Community, partly for the sake of limiting competition directly, but also to make the case that American bigness required European mergers, bigness, and especially deli-

3. Patrick M. Boarman, *Germany's Economic Dilemma* (New Haven, Yale University Press, 1964), pp. 189 ff. The same view is taken by Octave Gélinier in *Morale de l'enterprise et destin de la nation,* (Paris, Plon, 1965) and noted approvingly by Servan-Schreiber, p. 53.

cacy in administering the antitrust provisions of the European Economic Community.[4] The Union des Industries de la Communauté Européenne, representing industrialists throughout the Common Market, complains of the effects of American investors in bidding up the prices of inputs, especially capital, and lowering the prices of outputs. It dislikes certain sales methods adopted by American companies in Europe. A statement by the organization said, "American companies were often 'misinformed' about the price structures existing in European markets. Americans . . . tended to provoke price wars."[5]

It would be inappropriate to dismiss all these arguments. Foreign firms operating in Europe, backed by the financial power of an overseas parent, can take chances with undercapitalization, for example, which would be excessively risky for local competitors who must rely on their own resources.[6] But many of the arguments in the catalog which follow are mere rationalizations of unhappiness at new entry into old if rapidly growing markets. Where politicians fulminate at the political aspects of direct investment in Europe and warn against Europe being "colonized by foreign participations, inventions, and capabilities," to quote President De Gaulle's New Year message for 1965, businessmen are moved by more intensive competition and prospectively lower profits. The intruder has some advantage that the local entrepreneur lacks, and this is universally regarded as unfair. Or the intruder is muscling into cartelized territory, as in

4. *New York Times* (July 28, 1965), p. 16.

5. "U.S. Investment: A European View," *New York Times* (March 15, 1967).

6. Thus, for example, I.B.M. in 1966 had a 3.5 quick asset ratio at home and a 1.5 ratio in its foreign operations.

the case of American penetration into German banking, securities distribution, and finance of various sorts. Hermann J. Abs, the distinguished president of the Deutsche Bank, deserves careful hearing when he pronounces on most economic subjects. When he pronounces on foreign investment by banks, or foreign industrial investment supported by foreign sources of capital which thereby escape German surveillance, however, it is useful to make allowance for his natural reluctance to see German banking arrangements, which give great power to a few banks, disturbed by foreign competition.

Foreign Firms Do Not Know How to Behave

Two early episodes in the checkered career of recent United States investment in France were the closing by General Motors of its Frigidaire plant at Gennevilliers, and some layoffs at Remington Rand near Lyon.[7] The Frigidaire plant had been producing a large American model which was too big for the normal French household, and Italian imports of a properly designed and much cheaper model made the Gennevilliers plant unprofitable. The provision of such competition was what the Common Market was supposed to do. But there was a French uproar when the five hundred or so workers were laid off. This was not the French way of doing things, despite the fact that there was brimful employment and the employees easily got other good positions.[8] French regulations continue to make it difficult to release

7. Allan W. Johnstone, *United States Direct Investment in France* (Cambridge, Mass., M.I.T. Press, 1965), p. 14.
8. One press story states that the French oppose closing any plant, "no matter how uneconomic." "Europe Flexing Merger Muscles," *New York Times* (March 3, 1966).

men from jobs, requiring notice to the authorities, sev-
erance pay, and so forth, through the tightest labor market conditions, when the usual economic view would be
that it was desirable to transfer workers from less to more
productive work. There is even a hint of political dema-
goguery in the episode. A General Motors executive who
worked in France at the time told me that the other jobs
had been found for the workers but that a French cabinet
minister had seen fit to make an outcry to capture head-
lines. The exact merits of the dispute are difficult to ap-
praise from a distance, and Johnstone supports the
French side. But it is hard to take seriously the charge of
American cruelty in discharging redundant employees at
a time when labor was desperately short. The Remington
Rand episode was broadly similar.

The complaints are not confined to France. From all
countries comes criticism of high-handed methods that
fail to heed local practices and tradition. The most spec-
tacular recent episode concerns an American textile man-
ufacturer who closed down the Roberts-Arundel textile
machinery plant in Stockport, England, after a year-long
struggle to change methods of production, and even of
tea-making, against the resistance of the Amalgamated
Engineering Union. The American industrialist con-
fessed to having been naïve, and his troubles were compounded by running head-on into a struggle for the lead-
ership of what *The Economist* calls Britain's most reac-
tionary trade union.[9] Some change is inevitable, however, if the investor who sees an opportunity to make
profits by changing production and sales methods is to
succeed. Few companies can afford to take as long and

9. "Roberts-Arundel: Whose Failure?" *Economist*, 225, No. 6486
(December 16, 1967); and "American Boss Loses to Britons," *New
York Times* (January 4, 1968).

patient a view as did the Standard Oil Company of New Jersey when it spent two years altering trade union practice through negotiation in the interest of both efficiency and higher pay scale (but reduced employment) in its Fawley refinery.[10] Changes in economic practices should be applied with delicacy and finesse, but, in the best of circumstances, there will be violation of tradition and a sense of outrage.

Foreign Firms Escape the Commissariat au Plan

An initial French reaction against direct investment was that it escaped the control of the Commissariat au Plan. To ensure conformity to planned production, French planning authorities use official control of the capital market. The capital market is weak. Firms rely heavily on profits for investment, but, to the extent that outside funds are required, which is high in some industries and increases when profits are squeezed by costs rising faster than prices, firms must turn to the capital market. Here they run the official gauntlet. In early postwar days, investment funds were provided by the Fonds de Modernisation, equipped with Marshall Plan counterpart funds, derived from selling aid goods for francs. After aid came to an end, the flow of savings through savings banks into the centralized Caisse de Dépôts et Consignation provided the authorities with a major source of capital. Banque de France willingness to discount company paper, affecting banks' readiness to make advances to companies, provided another opportunity for the financial authorities to check to see whether the firm

10. Allan Flanders, *The Fawley Productivity Agreements: A Case Study of Management and Collective Bargaining* (London, Faber and Faber, 1964).

was behaving in ways approved by the Commissariat au Plan. In an indicative rather than an imperative planning system, where the Commissariat asked firms rather than telling them—merely pointing the way—control over access to investment capital has been a significant means of encouraging compliance. The foreign firm with access to capital outside France escaped this checkpoint.

But can the foreign firm really escape French industrial control? A new firm, it will be remembered, has to obtain permission in order to be able to undertake operations in France, despite the guarantee of national treatment to American firms in the Treaty of Friendship, Commerce, and Navigation between France and the United States renewed in 1959. This is one place where the French can check on what a foreign firm intends to do. Second, most firms in fact obtain the bulk of their capital locally: through borrowing, which is subject to the same surveillance as that of French firms (except to the extent that the larger foreign firm has a higher credit standing with French banks), or from profits, which equally enable French firms to escape official control. To the extent that the profits of foreign firms are higher than those of the locals, as my theory requires them to be, foreigners are less subject to constraint through need to borrow capital than their domestic competitors.

But there is more to the issue. In the first place, why is control wanted? If the Commissariat au Plan is interested in growth, it should presumably bless the efforts of firms to risk their own money in expanded production. The Commissariat has, from time to time, believed that there was too much production in automobiles, detergents, electricity, and similar industries—and has often been demonstrated to have been wrong in these fears. If the Commissariat gradually loses its belief in expansion and growth and slips into an attitude of fear of overproduction and falling prices, there is reason for it to want to hold back foreigners, particularly those that are more efficient than French firms. But this is to adopt the competitive fears of the Confédération du Patronat Français, which are generally regarded in France as Malthusian and antigrowth.

Second, and more important, foreign companies in Europe are hardly likely to defy authoritative direction, and above all not when it has a reasonable case. French authorities have enforced some mergers between French and American companies, which the Americans were most unwilling to engage in, but realistically did enter. American firms may be reluctant to undertake particular investments wanted by the Commissariat if they believe them to be unprofitable or unsuitable for their interests and skills. But control of external capital supply is a negative restraint, not a positive stimulus, and where the authorities clearly oppose something contemplated by an outside firm, and for understandable reasons, they have only to drop a hint.

The Need to Keep Independent of American Technology

Belgium and Italy, as I have indicated, want American technology as an aid to breaking out of an industrial structure that includes a number of industries where technology is frozen. The French attitude is more complex. In lines where they have hardly made a beginning —as years ago in the nuclear energy field, or more recently in electronic circuitry—they welcome ready-made technology from abroad, as a base to build on. Elsewhere, however, they want technological independence (or even to push the French standard abroad). To have the French technology overwhelmed from abroad is scientific slavery, or colonization by foreign inventions, against which President De Gaulle has spoken eloquently.

There is more here than mere desire for prestige, but it is hard to determine how much. French technology is first class in many fields—in railroading, jet aircraft (like the Caravelle, Mirage, and Mystère), high-voltage electricity transmission, automobile design (as in the Citroën), and one could go on. In most industries, perhaps, technological standards are not interconnected, and perfect competition in engineering design and performance is desirable. But in many fields, there are external economies to standardization. This was originally true at the national level; as trade and travel expand, it is increasingly so at the international.

The difficulty is that the first in a given field sets the standard, and it is economic for others to adopt it. In addition, when an original standard becomes obsolete, the more widely it has been adopted, the more difficult and expensive it is to change it to a better one. There is a short-term loss from failing to adopt the widely used technology; there may be a long-term gain from adopting and ultimately disseminating a superior technological standard. This is the infant-industry argument. But infant industries do not always grow to manhood, and the independent technology with its short-term loss may turn out to be an also-ran with long-term wastage of resources.

Moreover, the French resistance to foreign technology where standardization is economic is not altogether based on the infant-industry argument. In part it is a matter of prestige, and even of politics or nationalism. I am unable to pass judgment on the merits of the several systems of color television, but it does seem curious that the French and Russians alone have adopted the French system, instead of the American-German. Even if the French is better, there is doubt that it is enough better to make up for the loss of compatibility with the international standard. But the French will argue that if theirs is better, the world should convert to it, not they to the world's standard. The point is understandable, but it is reminiscent of the Great Western Railroad's fight in England at the end of the last century to resist the standard gauge in railroad tracks because it had the better wide gauge. Ultimately it lost, and the cost of transshipping from standard to wide gauge during the forty-year struggle was a continuous burden. One can cite also the difficult decisions to change from right- to left-hand drive in automotive traffic, made by Czechoslovakia, Austria, and Sweden, but resisted still by Britain, Australia, and New Zealand; and above all the different standards of electric voltage for home consumption in Europe and the United States, and of electrical sockets which so baffle and frustrate the transoceanic resident.

The case for standardization gets stronger as the world gets smaller: the pitch of the screw thread harmonized by Britain and the United States; decimalization in Australia, New Zealand, and ultimately Britain, despite the superiority of the duodecimal system in some ultimate sense; the adoption of metric measurement—very slowly to be sure—in the United States and England; publication of scientific papers in English without translation in Scandinavian, Dutch, German, Swiss, and Italian periodicals, and even the production of native scientific work in English. It is frustrating to the French who have a beautiful and precise language—though one perhaps not as versatile as Frenchmen believe—to have their language invaded by English and American, or to detect an asymmetry in international meetings in that delegates are expected to know English, but that all other languages have to be translated.[11] But standardization is economical, and transformers, converters, translators, even driving on the left in a left-hand-drive car, expensive. There is surely a series of trade-offs between the capital costs of converting to the best standards and the current loss from failing to standardize. The rate of interest will play a major role in the calculation. What is awkward is that we lack supply curves suggesting how expensive it is to seek the prestige of keeping to national standards (with an estimated chance of having the national ultimately adopted as the international standard), or demand curves which say how much of other things we are willing to give up to keep our standards national.

Prestige is a curious commodity; its possession is not nourishing, but its absence is debilitating. It is, moreover, elusive, accruing in economic fields to those who are successful in the pursuit of practical goals—economic growth, efficient resource allocation, a new technique that enables a certain task to be performed, or an equilibrium exchange rate—but vanishing before those who seek ends for the prestige they convey. "Science for science's sake" or science for making a better mousetrap is likely to bring prestige, while "science for prestige's sake" will surely not.

In a new book, a young political scientist raises a more profound question about international technology.[12] It

11. But Etiemble in *Parlez-Vous Franglez?* (Paris, Gallimard, 1964) surely weakens his case by overstating it. It is poignant that Louis Armand, the French industrialist, in discussing direct investment should mention as an aside, "It is difficult to forget the colonies, and French, the diplomatic language." See Servan-Schreiber, pp. 200–01.

12. Robert Gilpin, *France in the Age of the Scientific State* (Princeton, Princeton University Press, 1968).

is regarded by President De Gaulle, he believes, as a threat to the nation-state. This is partly for reasons of defense, which lead France to fence off military and some other sensitive areas—atomic energy, computers, space, and selected chemical and electronic industries—from foreign investment. But it goes beyond it. France (Servan-Schreiber would say Europe) as an entity requires an independent or competitive technology to be a world power. Switzerland and Sweden can become wealthy by carving out small pieces of international industrial technology and specializing in them. This model is rich in special possibilities, but it is not open to, say, France, which wants world rank and must, therefore, compete technologically over the full line of significant activity. If Europe fails to meet the American challenge and becomes autonomous in these matters, it may go the way of the Arab into fatalism, collectivism, impotence, and become a satellite of the United States.[13]

It is difficult to know how to react to this quasi-mystical attitude. There is something in it. Certainly the United States has reacted strongly to the Russian effort in space, and is reacting to the Anglo-French project to build a supersonic transport, the *Concorde*. The United States government pushes United States standards in military equipment, telecommunications, aircraft and missile guidance, and so forth. Where one nation pushes, it is reasonable to expect another nation to resist. It may well be that the technological lead of the United States colors and distorts the view from these shores as to the wastefulness of maintaining an independent technology for its own sake as contrasted with maintaining a different because a better technology.

13. Servan-Schreiber, esp. pp. 111, 162, 171, 191 ff.

Nevertheless, I find it hard to fault the Swiss and Swedish example. Is this "bitter mediocrity" (a phrase of President De Gaulle's)? Sweden affects and is affected by international technological standards. One thousand Swedish companies in seventy countries employ 200,000 workers.[14] They neither dominate foreign countries, however, nor are they dominated. The reciprocal relationship would seem satisfactory in the abstract. The De Gaulle viewpoint suggests a hunger for power, a need for France to dominate. This, from a United States author, may merely be the pot and the kettle. Perhaps I have wandered too far from economic territory into the morass of politics. It is never possible to avoid the political for long, but let us return to higher, dry and familiar ground.

Distortion of Export Patterns

The principal burden of defending the international corporation against the accusation widely leveled at it, that it refuses to allow its subsidiaries to export, will be saved for the next lecture and the discussion of the attitudes of Canada, Australia, and New Zealand. But the issue is not absent from the European discussion. It arose in the discussion of the Ford takeover of the minority shares of Ford of Dagenham in 1960, and has been discussed in Norway. Nor is the Ford defense, that it exports a lot from Dagenham, persuasive, since one would have to know how much the company would have exported if it had been British owned and controlled. On the whole, however, the shoe is on the other foot. It is not firms that distort efficient allocations, but government.

14. See "New Paths for Sweden," *Economist, 225,* No. 6478 (special survey, October 28, 1967).

The prospect of the Common Market in the mid-1950s led economists to expect two effects on foreign investment: first, the new investment response of outsiders to trade diversion against imports from outside the European Economic Community; and second, the rearrangement of existing investment within the area in response to the widening of the internal market. Call these investment creation (stimulated by trade diversion) and investment diversion (stimulated by internal trade creation). I have argued that the Common Market may have produced more new investment (investment creation) through calling attention to a growing European market which had lain unnoticed over the horizon of foreign producers than it did by altering fine calculations of the most profitable choice between shipping from the outside or producing in situ. But while the investment-creation response was substantial for whatever reason—or substantially overdone as viewed by many quarters in Europe and by the United States Treasury Department—investment diversion has been on a moderate scale.

The point has been made that foreign firms are more European than domestic European companies. Like Mediterranean labor which lacks roots in northern Europe, it is highly mobile. If the removal of the tariff between France and its partners draws French firms from the south and west to the north and east, an American firm has no compunction about letting itself be drawn clear across the border. If the internal tariff barriers of the Common Market caused a distortion of efficient economic allocation, their removal provided the opportunity for reallocation.

In the event, however, investment diversion did not go so far. In Europe in the summer of 1964 I heard the slogan of one American firm, "To sell in France, produce in France"—despite the Common Market. And the same seemed to hold for most other countries. Some of the large increase in post-1950 international trade may well have been the deliberate moving of materials between plants of the same company across national lines, as American companies yielded to the pressure of host governments to spread their investments for optimum political rather than efficient economic siting. It is said that in one year the foreign trade of Belgium rose more than 20 percent on both exports and imports, largely as a result of shipments to and fro between Ford of Cologne, Germany, and Ford of Belgium, plants which might more efficiently have been located closer together in either country.

The possibility that American firms are in a better position to adapt to economic stimuli because more flexible, and freer to move assets in and out of the countries of Europe, raises one appalling thought. Suppose that competition in the European automobile industry goes the way of that in the United States, and reduces some 30 to 40 automobile companies to 3 or 4. It would be most awkward politically and emotionally if three of the survivors turned out to be General Motors, Ford, and Chrysler. These are the largest companies in the industry on a worldwide basis and are therefore able to take advantage of the economies of scale in research, designs for standardizing parts among different models, and long runs on fixed investments in jigs and dies. There has been talk of Volkswagen merging with Renault, or Renault with Fiat. Most mergers have been along national lines —Peugeot with Renault, or Volkswagen with Daimler-Benz—for limited purposes and not so thorough as to lose the identity or the management of the smaller company. Fiat cannot merge with a foreign company, I have been told, since it is a national monument. These national constraints on efficient allocation and merger for the sake of eliminating the redundant suggest a troubled period ahead.

It is possible then that international firms in Europe throttle potential exports of great value to one or another country. More likely, however, is that a strong residue of national citizenship by companies and protection by governments prevents optimal resource allocation and even produces a substantial volume of "exports" and "imports" of limited value for the economies concerned. On this showing American companies would like to take advantage of the Common Market to rationalize their European investments, produce from the most efficient sources, and export to other markets. They are prevented from so doing by the refusal to expand the Common Market to encompass Britain, Scandinavia, and the rest of the Outer Seven on the one hand; and on the other by the residue of the protectionist spirit among the Six which suggests that such a policy would be unwise.

Buying Our Plants with Our Money

One particular source of indignation in France is the thought that the United States has had a deficit and France a surplus in their respective balances of payments, so that when a capital movement takes place from the United States to France, the French have to accumulate dollars or gold.[15] In May 1965 the French financial au-

15. Cf. the excerpt from the unofficial translation of remarks made at President De Gaulle's press conference of November 27, 1967 (*New York Times*, November 28, 1967):

It is true that there is an American foothold in some of our business enterprises. But we know that this is due in large part not so much to organic superiority of the United States as to

thorities undertook to convert all dollar holdings beyond working balances into gold, so that thereafter the claim could be made that the United States was buying real assets in France for gold. Prior to this change in policy, the reaction was that the French were required to lend the United States the money to buy their plants.

This accusation is analytically bound up with a German complaint, that American direct investors cause inflation by bidding up prices, especially of labor but also of materials, plant, and equipment. It is assumed in both ways of looking at American investment that the country in question is in macroeconomic equilibrium, with savings equal to investment at an appropriate level of full employment. Along comes incremental investment from outside the system. In the German case, the transfer process is initiated with incomes and prices rising. Since there is already full employment, the process is inflationary. In France, on the other hand, investment is not allowed to rise. This would disturb domestic stability. In consequence, added investment by the United States must be matched by a reduction of investment or added savings elsewhere in the system. Income is not allowed to rise

---

the dollar inflation they export to others under cover of the gold-exchange standard.

It is quite remarkable that the total of the American balance-of-payments deficit for the last eight years is precisely the same as the total for American investment in Western European countries.

There is obviously an outside element, artificial and unilateral, weighing on our national patrimony. And it is well known that France would like to see an end to this abuse, in the interests of the whole world, even in the interests of the United States, for which the balance-of-payments deficit and the inflation are deplorable just as they are for everybody else.

and spill over into imports, transfer is impossible, and the exchange from abroad ends up in foreign-exchange reserves.

It must be admitted that this analysis may fit actual circumstances. Assume that both the United States and France are in monetary and expenditure equilibrium, with balanced international payments, and the United States wantonly or carelessly expands its money supply, lowers interest rates, and generates a new capital investment to France. Interest rates tend to decline in France, but the monetary authorities sterilize the inflow to prevent inflation. The American investment goes forward. Some French investment gets repressed. And the result of the repression is that the dollar exchange accumulates.

This model assumes that the United States is inflationary and Europe (France) is not. It is a fact, however, that between 1960 and 1966 European prices were rising much faster than those in the United States. It is sometimes said that the United States had no inflation because it exported it to Europe, but it is hard to make sense out of such a statement. With both the United States and Europe at full employment, monetary expansion in the United States would produce inflation first in the United States, and only secondarily in Europe, except under extraordinary assumptions, such as a very kinked marginal physical product curve of capital in the United States but not in Europe, implying that at a slightly lower rate of interest there were no further investment opportunities in the United States but a great many across the Atlantic.

But the real argument against the model is its assumption that the American direct investment is the autonomous variable that supervenes after everything else is in stable equilibrium. Suppose it is, instead, the most profitable investment in France. On our showing, it is something that the French cannot themselves do, or they would have done it. If it is an inframarginal investment —not necessarily, to be sure, the first one—there is a transfer or a disequilibrium problem unless the French inflate to adjust relative prices to the exchange rate, or adjust the exchange rate to relative prices. It is as correct to say that the franc exchange rate is undervalued in relation to prices (or prices are too low for the exchange rate) as it is to blame the balance-of-payments difficulties on an arbitrary and quixotic movement of direct investment.

In general equilibrium it is almost always wrong to ascribe particular results to particular causes, and especially is this true in the balance of payments where all the items in the balance and in underlying costs, prices, income, money supply, and so forth, determine each other.

Liquidity Preference

This is the general case. A special case within it is worth examination. It constitutes an exception to the general theory that direct investment is not so much a capital movement as an effort to take advantage of particular opportunities, open to the investing firm but not to local business. Capital movements will normally be undertaken by financial rather than business institutions. But in the 1960s, the financial links between capital markets were disrupted first by the Interest Equalization Tax (I.E.T.) of July 1963, and then by the Gore amendment applying the tax to long-term bank loans. As interest rates rose in Europe relative to those in the United States because these financial connections between the two markets were broken, international firms increasingly found themselves responding to financial rather than business stimuli. Whereas in the general case, direct investment occurs because of differences in I in the formula for discounting a stream of income $\left(C = \dfrac{I}{r} \right)$, after the middle of 1964, more and more direct investment had financial aspects, or was a response to differences in r.

Assume a situation in which the marginal physical product of capital is the same in all uses on both sides of the Atlantic, but that some European country—call it France—has a different structure of interest rates than the United States because of a strong preference of its savers for keeping their capital in liquid form. Assume further that the normal interconnections between capital markets provided by a joined bond market and joined markets for short-term capital are not functioning. If we assume that French savers want to keep their savings liquid, and French borrowers want to fund their liabilities over a longer period of time than sight loans, long-term rates of interest will be higher and short-term rates lower in France than in the United States. American investors will be willing to pay higher prices for given investments, new or already existing, than French buyers. Some of this investment will take the form of bonds if foreign investors are willing and permitted to hold French securities, and French companies are willing to issue long-term debt. But if the bond markets of the two countries are fenced off from one another, financial intermediation can take place in real assets or direct investment.

Suppose on the basis of this greater preference for liquidity in France than in the United States that an American firm buys out an existing French concern. There is a temptation in France to make a distinction between takeovers and new assets, but this is by and large invalid: where the investment is based on an advantage, the French owner sells out because the American pays him more than the assets are worth to him at his existing rate of profit.[16] Where the investment is made on the basis of liquidity preference, the productivity of the assets is the same to both entrepreneurs, but the American is willing to pay a price at which the latter converts the assets into cash.

If it is the seller himself who has the high liquidity preference, he is happier, and therefore closer to his long-run equilibrium, with cash than with real assets. The American has gained a factory, but the French seller has achieved liquidity. If he chose to hold his liquidity in dollars, there would be no problem. The American and the French exchange dollars for plant. If the seller prefers francs, as is the normal expectation, someone else must hold the dollars and allow him to hold francs. This could be the banking system; if the banks are unwilling to hold dollars, it must be the central bank. But there is no use in the central bank's complaining. It always had the choice of providing liquidity to the market to satisfy its demand at the rates of interest prevailing abroad. With given interest rates and liquidity preferences an American investor can pay a higher price than any Frenchman is willing to pay. The French owner sells out because his cash is low and his access to credit limited.

16. There is one sense in which it is appropriate to welcome new investments but to prohibit takeovers, and that concerns monopoly. In an industry with five or less firms, for example, a newly established firm adds to competition, whereas a takeover does not. But this has not been the traditional objection to take-overs by such politicos as Michel Debré. Rather they reflect the more simple-minded view that a new investment adds something, whereas a takeover merely buys out something that already existed.

It is extreme to assume that the original owner had the demand for liquidity. But to modify this makes no difference to the analysis. Assume that the original owner sells out because the price offered is more than the plant is worth to him. He then buys or builds another plant. If he buys another plant, the same question arises: Did the new seller sell for cash to hold, and why? But if he builds, is it appropriate to assume that the new investment is incremental? If it is, this puts pressure on incomes, prices, costs, imports, and so forth to start the transfer process. But if liquidity preference is high in the system, it is likely that the rise in costs and prices induces some investor just on the margin of deciding whether to part with liquidity in exchange for plant and equipment to conclude that the game is too dangerous and to postpone his undertaking. In this instance increased investment by the direct investor, or by one of the succession of entrepreneurs who build new plants with the proceeds of the sale of the old, is offset by a reduction of investment elsewhere in the system. The failure of the transfer mechanism is the result of liquidity preference in France. The American investor has exchanged liquidity for the plant, which suits a French seller. If the French authorities do not approve the result, they have the option of making the wanted liquidity available to the economy themselves.

I thus demur at the view that American investors have purchased French plants with money borrowed from the Bank of France. The analysis, if not wrong, is at least incomplete. In the usual case, where the direct investment is based on the possession of some advantage over French investors, the balance-of-payments surplus in France represents the failure of transfer to take place. This surplus is the result of total macroeconomic policies, including

monetary, fiscal, and exchange-rate policies. One cannot
blame the balance-of-payments disequilibrium on direct
investment. If the investment arises from differences in
liquidity preference in the United States and France,
there are two ways to regard it. The direct investment
would be eliminated if the French authorities provided
the liquidity the system needs. If they refuse to provide it
themselves, and at the same time retain their connections
with the international capital market, they can hardly
complain that it is provided from abroad. When this is
done, the foreign provider of liquidity will invest long
and borrow short, and the economy provided with
liquidity will borrow long and lend short. This is trade
in liquidity and not in real assets. It occurs with even
partially integrated capital markets. If it is not wanted,
the answer is to break all links between the capital
markets. This means foreign-exchange control.

A brilliant young French economist objects to the emphasis on liquidity preference in this analysis, saying
instead that French capital has been monetized in the
American capital market. This market is dominated by
an oligopoly of a dozen great banks which, with economies of scale, can charge lower interest rates than European banks.[17] The distinction seems to me verbal. International financial intermediation takes place for reasons
of scale economies in the larger market, or higher liquidity preference in the smaller, or both. What is significant
is that the balance-of-payments deficit is a monetary result of joined capital markets, on top of a transferred
amount of real capital. It can be eliminated only by

17. Serge-Christophe Kolm, "La Monétization Américaine du
Capital Français," *Révue économique, 18,* No. 6 (November 1967),
pp. 1038–57.

breaking up the connections between the capital markets
—and all the connections, not just most of them; or by
improving the efficiency of the smaller market, or altering
its liquidity preference, until it matches that of the
larger. The "remarkable" coincidence between United
States direct investment in Europe and the balance-of-
payments deficit of the last eight years does not signify
causality.

Note that the European central banks end up with
dollars even when the United States direct investor borrows directly in the local capital market—a case where
one could truly say that the United States borrows the
money from Europe to buy their assets. The local borrowing in Europe tightens interest rates further; some
marginal borrowers (but not lenders) transfer their operations from the local to the international market (New
York, but after the escalating restrictions, the Euro-dollar
and Euro-dollar bond markets). The dollars are sold
against local currency for use in Europe. There is no
one to hold them except the central bank. Europe has
borrowed long on private account and loaned short on
official. This is a balance-of-payments "surplus." Directly
or through the Euro-dollar market, the United States
ends up lending long and borrowing short, a "deficit"—
normal enough as financial intermediation in the domestic financial markets, but not yet accepted in international dealing.

Nationalism and Direct Investment: The Japanese Case

I suspect, though it is impossible to prove it one way
or another, that the basic reason against foreign direct
investment is fear of foreign competition, and the general form it takes in nationalism, disguised as a rule with

highly rationalized arguments. The infant-industry argument, as I have said, is a good one, but often misused. In all but the infant-industry case the nationalistic argument against foreign investment cannot be gainsaid. The only question is what exclusion costs.

French ambivalence, which has led that country to argue against direct investment in general but to accept most particular applications, first grudgingly, and later with more alacrity, is instructive. So too is the Japanese example.

Japan is the country which par excellence has resisted foreign investment.[18] Prior to 1900 it resisted all investment. When foreign borrowing was undertaken in the early twentieth century it took the form of bonds, largely funneled through the Industrial Bank of Japan, which limited contact between domestic debtors and foreign creditors. After World War II the Foreign Investment Law of 1950 restricted foreign borrowing for fear that the Japanese balance of payments would be weakened. United States aid made it possible for a time to dispense with private funds. This law authorized foreign investment only when "foreign capital investment contributes to the attainment of self-sufficiency and the healthy development of the Japanese economy and also to the improvement of Japan's balance-of-payments situation."

About 1956 Japanese concerns sought to license foreign patents and technology on a larger scale. The bal-

18. See S. Okita and T. Miki, "Treatment of Foreign Capital—A Case Study for Japan," in J. H. Adler, ed., *Capital Movements, Proceedings of a Conference Held by the International Economic Association* (New York, St. Martin's Press, 1967), pp. 139–74; and E. P. Reubens, "Foreign Capital and Domestic Development in Japan," in Simon Kuznets, ed., *Economic Growth, Brazil, India, Japan* (Durham, N.C., Duke University Press, 1955).

ance of payments improved, import liberalization took place, and a demand arose for liberalization of inward capital movements. Since 1959 the Foreign Investment Law has been relaxed on several occasions. In 1965, foreign capital was given access to Japan so long as it did not (1) put excessive pressure on small-sized industries (the competitive motive for restriction); (2) seriously disturb industrial order (ditto); and (3) seriously impede the development of new industrial techniques recently commercialized or about to be commercialized (infant-industry protection). The Japanese government still favors the issuance of bonds, or the contraction of loans. It recognizes, however, that where a Japanese firm wants to import technology, it may be necessary to admit venture capital. In addition, it is judged advisable to respond to political pressure from domestic interests seeking foreign capital assistance and from the Organization for Economic Cooperation and Development, which urged liberalization, largely at United States insistence.

The result has been, so far as can be judged from meager press reports in the United States, a threefold program of retreat: with substantial liberalization promised for the future—in 1971; 100 percent foreign ownership of equities allowed now in the strongest Japanese industries where the chances for foreign success seem virtually nonexistent—steel, cement, motorcycles, cotton and synthetic fiber spinning—plus no more than 50 percent in a long list of other industries; and case-by-case liberalization where considerations of bargaining power require it. Thus where foreign technology is particularly sought after but unavailable under licensing because the foreign owner insists on exploiting its scarcity himself, permission to acquire a substantial equity in a Japanese company will be given; and the same may be done where the initial investment experiences losses that the Japanese shareholders are incapable of sustaining.[19] It should be noted that the trend toward liberalization weakens Japanese short-run bargaining power and strengthens that of the foreign investor.

Whether Japanese liberalization owes more to United States pressure or to the need to admit foreign capital in order to obtain its advantages is impossible for the outsider to judge. That Japan held out so long is probably owing to its special advantages—a high rate of personal savings, technical ingenuity or virtuosity, and intense nationalism and discipline. The Japanese example appeals very much to nationalists elsewhere.[20]

But the Japanese experience is ambiguous. On the infant-industry score it is highly instructive. Japan was clearly right in postponing admission of foreign capital into automobiles until its own industry had shaken down into efficient producing and stable financial units—this admission is now scheduled for 1971. In other industries, however, licensing of technology and borrowing capital through debt seem to have promised too little growth. The true believer will ascribe the Japanese yielding to

19. Liberalization had barely begun in 1965 when the account of Okita and Miki ends. The further large steps in 1966 and 1967 have been pieced together from rather scrappy newspaper accounts. See especially "Heinz Seeks 80% of Japan Venture," *New York Times* (February 21, 1967); "Foreign Capital Helped by Japan," *New York Times* (May 31, 1967); and "Auto Production Gaining in Japan," *New York Times* (February 11, 1968).

20. See "France Stresses Atom Deterrent," *New York Times* (January 30, 1968), in which President De Gaulle suggested that Japan should follow the French example in seeking an independent nuclear deterrent. The short section on the Japanese example in Servan-Schreiber's *Le Défi Américain* (French edition of *The American Challenge*, pp. 303–07), however, is not very communicative.

arm-twisting by the aggressive capitalism of the United States. Such pressure existed, and it achieved liberalization for United States capitalists to start 100 percent motorcycle companies in Japan in competition with Honda and Suzuki. A more complimentary explanation, and my instincts suggest a more accurate one, is that Japan arrived at the conclusion that the maintenance of a modern economy requires access to some specialized technology on the terms on which it is available. To maintain complete independence from foreign enterprise is to fall behind economically. Either decision may be taken, to be sure, as economic independence is weighed against economic growth. Japan seems to have decided in favor of growth.

Ambivalence

Ambivalence about direct investment is normal. Most of us want to have our cake and eat it too, to get the benefit of foreign technology and capital, but not to share control of our industry. But economics teaches that the answer to "Which do you choose?" cannot be "Both." If technology is a scarce resource, available only on terms of admitting equity capital, the government of a country may devote its own resources to producing an equivalent or substitute technology (as the French are doing in the nuclear field), accept the terms, or go without. There can, of course, be bargaining, so that it may be useful to appear to produce the equivalent or to be ready to go without in an effort to improve the terms on which the technology is ultimately obtained from abroad. Some ambivalence may represent the technique of the tourist, walking away in feigned disdain from the bazaar. Bargaining technique aside, however, ambiva-

lence is likely to be the consequence of trying to weigh
political independence against economic advantage—a
task that requires establishing a *numéraire* in which they
can be compared, either a money price on the degree of
political independence that would be compromised to
compare with the income in money terms, or, still more
elusive, a political equivalent of the economic growth
sought or forgone. It is understandable that these valuations are likely to be highly subjective and erratic, which
means that the comparison comes out differently when
undertaken by rather similar observers, or by the same
observer on successive tries.

Leave aside the extreme cases—of defense industries
at one end and, say, breakfast foods or pickles at the
other. Let us also neglect the interconnections among decisions, and particularly the setting of precedents. Consider, rather, an industry such as oil. How important is
it to buy one's oil from a company or companies owned
by nationals? British, American, and French interests
have fought in the international arena, with the help of
governments, to establish international oil companies.
The greater success of two British (Shell and British
Petroleum) and five American (Jersey, Mobil, Texas,
California, and Gulf) companies has led the French to
push in the Middle East and North Africa, and to defend
the French market by limiting foreign penetration of it.
Belgium, perhaps the European country most friendly to
American investment, resisted an attempt to take over
Petrofina. The issue is most sharply put in connection
with the possible takeover of the distributing company
Aral, in an editorial in *Die Zeit* entitled "A Powerful
Industrial Nation Without a Viable Oil Company":

> . . . nationalistic phraseology is therefore out of
> place, but so is any short-sighted provincial ap-

proach. To dispense with an internationally viable oil concern is to abandon a reliable source of foreign exchange and technical expertise. Furthermore the country would be deprived of a broad basis for the development of its petrochemical industry, of the findings of much basic research and—what is not to be disparaged today—of political influence in the world.[21]

The foreign-exchange and research reasons need not be dealt with: Germany's balance of payments flourishes with assistance from other quarters, and her chemical research using oil and coal-tar stocks has long existed on the basis of foreign-owned companies. The basic question is political, and its answer is ambiguous. Nationalism is out of place; one must not be provincial. Is it possible to be economically powerful, without having (and exercising) political influence? How does one choose between economic welfare and political power when they are sometimes alternatives (in the weak) and sometimes complements (in the strong)?

21. See *The German Tribune,* No. 204 (February 26, 1966), p. 13.

United States Direct Investment in the Dominions

There is perhaps no valid organizing principle for devoting a separate chapter to United States direct investment in Australia, Canada, and New Zealand—not all the Dominions of the Commonwealth, it will be noted, but the major ones. The issues treated in the previous lectures—technology, transfer pricing, and taxation, not to mention monopoly and money—apply to the Dominions as well as to Europe. So will some issues reserved for the less developed countries and the lecture to follow. But the Dominions are a convenient peg on which to hang a continuation of the discussion. They have recently been the subject of four outstanding contributions to the literature.[1] They stand between the developed countries of Europe and the less developed countries of Africa, Asia, and Latin America, rapidly growing but in great need of capital. They are sparsely populated, highly educated, and with similarities and differences

1. Donald T. Brash, *American Investment in Australian Industry;* A. E. Safarian, *Foreign Ownership of Canadian Industry;* R. S. Deane, "Foreign Investment in New Zealand Manufacturing" (unpublished doctoral dissertation at the Victoria University of Wellington, N.Z., submitted November 1967); *Foreign Ownership and the Structure of Canadian Industry,* Report of the Task Force on the Structure of Canadian Industry, prepared for the Privy Council Office (Ottawa, Queen's Printer, January 1968).

economically and politically and in their reaction to the common problem of foreign direct investment.

The problems chosen for this discussion could be shifted without much loss of logic either above to Europe or below to the less developed countries. Their treatment here is to this extent arbitrary. But we discuss first the question whether certain areas of the host economy should be prohibited to foreign exploitation, and in particular natural resources, communications, banking, and soft drinks; second, the contention that foreign investment is expensive, both in terms of profit rates and of the host country's balance of payments; third, whether direct investment distorts exports and imports; and last, whether direct investment compromises national independence, and if so, how far this can be mitigated by requirements of publicity and of representation of citizens of the host country among management, directors, and shareholders.

Natural Resources

There is an element of the peasant in all of us, with a special feeling for the good earth, not to mention the territorial imperative. We instinctively feel our land should be reserved for our people. Sweden and Norway regulate the foreign right to own real property, and in the latter country, especially forests, mines, and waterfalls.[2] The less developed countries pushed through the United Nations General Assembly a resolution reaffirming "the inalienable right of all countries to exercise permanent sovereignty over their natural resources in the interest of their national development, in conformity

2. Arthur Stonehill, *Foreign Ownership in Norwegian Enterprises* (Oslo, Central Bureau of Statistics, 1965), p. 28.

with the spirit and principles of the Charter of the United Nations."[3]

The laws of many countries (e.g. Mexico) reserve mining rights for the state, presumably so as to prevent the appropriation by private interests of the national heritage.

Any foreign purchase of an asset may be objected to because it takes place under monopsonistic conditions. The infant-industry argument is also applicable, making it a mistake to sell an asset today because it is worth more to foreigners than to nationals of the host country, if the time will come, presumably soon if the rate of interest is not very low, when domestic buyers will have overcome their disadvantage vis-à-vis the overseas purchaser, in which case they can afford to outbid him for the asset. There can also be a protectionist or redistributive element in objecting to foreign bidding up of a factor of production that domestic interests want cheaply. But apart from these three valid arguments, which apply to any asset and not just to natural resources, there is nothing in the argument that foreigners hurt us when they buy our land, or perhaps, as an American, I should say nothing in the argument that we Americans hurt them when our nationals buy their land.

If a willing buyer faces a willing seller under conditions of competition, no long-run declining costs, nor any policy for redistribution, the seller is paid the value of the property at that point in time. If it should be worth more in the future, the potential gain could be equal to, greater than, or less than the rate of compound interest on other assets. If equal, he will be just as well off with cash as with the physical asset—better according

3. Resolution 2148 (XXI) of November 25, 1966, adopted with no negative votes and six abstentions.

to revealed preference since he chose to sell. If less, he will evidently be better off to have sold. If the increment in value of the asset would be greater if he had held on, it must be because of lack of knowledge, which violates the assumption of perfect competition, or long-run decreasing costs which are also contrary to initial assumptions.

It makes no difference whether the asset is depletable like mines and oil wells, unchanged like a waterfall, or renewable and even improvable like forests and agricultural land. If the asset is depletable, the foreigner, if he is sensible, will provide depletion allowances to maintain the value of his capital, and possibly even its form, by capitalizing exploration expense for similar assets of equal value. But if it is nonrenewable, and depletion allowances cannot be used to duplicate it, the value of the capital can be preserved, if not the form, by using up the asset and investing depletion allowances in other capital assets. This is conservation in use. It is economic nonsense to fail to use capital assets because they cannot be replaced in the exact form, unless, of course, their value is appreciating each year at a rate in excess of the rate of interest. But in this last case, the domestic owner can sell the asset to a foreigner at a price that will reflect the fact that annual appreciation (an income item) is in excess of the rate of interest (the same in both countries, assuming perfect capital markets); and the foreigner, like a native owner, will hold the natural resource unused until the annual appreciation declines to the level of the rate of interest. If the asset is renewable or improvable like land, the foreigner can maintain his asset in the same or even better productive shape by reinvesting depreciation or depreciation plus capital improvement.

Whether the foreigner maintains the natural resource

or reconstitutes its value as capital at home or abroad, however, makes no difference to the host country, for it has exchanged this capital for money capital which it can use to purchase other assets. Of course it may consume its money capital, but this cannot be blamed on the foreigner. In the ordinary case, it will invest it; and given its inability to work the natural resource as effectively as the foreign direct investor, it will invest it more productively than if it had tried to use the natural resource, plus the other capital it would have had to invest through its own nationals. If the price is right, it pays to sell, whether the asset is God-given or man-made.

There is a great deal to the argument that purchases of natural resources take place in uncompetitive markets, or even "markets" overlain with force or duress. The British gunboat in the harbor when D'Arcy got his first oil concession in Persia in 1902, if I remember the date correctly, conveys an air of market imperfection. Knowledge may be imperfect on the part of less developed countries. And the infant-industry argument may apply as a country with oil-bearing land in due course acquires the capital and technology, if not the foreign markets, to undertake production and even refining for itself. That takes time. It may be useful to sell only part of a country's natural resources to foreigners today, in the hope of being in a better position to develop them tomorrow. These arguments are relevant to the less developed countries discussed in the next lecture. They hardly apply to Canada, Australia, and New Zealand.

The argument does not apply in Canada where foreigners, primarily United States residents, own and control the major portion of the capital investment in petroleum and natural gas and mining and smelting. The authors of the Task Force Report understand that United

States control of these resources is sought to coordinate operations in resources with vertically integrated activities abroad. They note that resource-based industries produced $1.85 billion of exports for Canada in 1965, as against $655 million of imports (to which should be added the profit on the investments), but they observe that Canada may get higher prices from the monopolistically controlled sale than would be the case if it tried to exploit the resources itself.[4]

Australia is uneasy about foreign ownership and control of natural resources only to the extent of some worry about Japanese operations in the iron mines of northwest Australia, far removed from centers of Australian population. It wants Australian capital associated in these operations. It would seem to the uninformed outsider, however, that so long as the Australian tax commissioner watches the transfer prices at which the Japanese-owned mines sell to their parents and ensures that these prices are as close as possible to a competitive standard, Australian interests can hardly be hurt. It is normal that Japanese steel interests would want to coordinate the production, shipment, and consumption of the iron ore involved. Australian owners would have great difficulty in making any contribution to the company other than capital, which might better be invested in industries where they have greater opportunities to participate in decision-making.

But the episode that interested me most was the storm of protest that arose in the press and Parliament in New Zealand when it was reported that American interests proposed to buy 60,000 acres of undeveloped and unproductive land in a Maori reserve. This action, it was

4. Task Force, *Foreign Ownership and the Structure of Canadian Industry,* pp. 202–03, 135.

asserted, would "compromise New Zealand independence and deprive present and future generations of valuable natural assests."[5] R. Davis wrote: "If we let them get away with it we are just a pack of fools and will have to start packing our bags immediately." (The Press, June 17, 1966.) Ellen Hunt asked, "Is there any reason why the American government should not be able to make free use of the land, now that it belongs outright to American citizens?" (The Press, June 23, 1966.) "New Zealand for Young New Zealanders" asked a series of hypothetical questions including, "Are we already annexed by the United States without benefit of adoption formalities which would give us some family rights? What will be the lot of the Maori when the Americans have all the say?" (The Press, June 23, 1966.)

Farm organizations, and especially the Young Farmers' Clubs, oppose action that raises the price of farmland which young farmers want to buy. It was suggested that the government buy the land and hold it in a reserve or develop it for subsequent sale to young farmers. One testy letter from M.G.H. (The Press, June 24, 1966) is explicit on the point: "In the South Island very many young men strongly desire to buy land but the price has risen so high that they are prevented from doing so. They would gladly take up undeveloped land if they could obtain tenure at a reasonable price. The Government has made the situation still worse by limiting the possibilities of borrowing money . . ." The first part of the quotation is covered by the analysis of sectional interests. Existing and aspiring farmers have different interests as to the price of land, and protection for the would-be

5. See the letter by "Ergo Tua Rura Manebunt" in The Press (Christchurch, N.Z., June 23, 1966). Other letters are in editions between June 17 and June 24, 1966.

farmer takes place at the expense of the owner of the land, in this case the government. Limited credit facilities raise a different issue, in which direct investment would be a consequence not of the greater capacity of the American interests to develop the land, but of imperfection of the international market for capital to which American interests have access but young farmers do not. If there were a sudden contraction of credit which pushed land on the market, there might be a question whether to allow foreigners to take advantage of bargain prices made available through distress selling.

In general, however, while the economist understands the peasant in each of us, including economists, he must reproach the peasant as a nationalist who generally does not think very clearly on the subject of foreign ownership. The question of extraterritoriality will occupy us later. It is not involved in the purchase of Maori reserve, which obviously remained under New Zealand sovereignty. There is something, but very little, to the infant-industry, monopoly, and redistributional arguments. For the most part, the instinct that makes us rush to prohibit foreign ownership of natural resources is based on the fallacy of misplaced concreteness. Natural resources are capital. As such, they qualify for foreign ownership. Whether to sell them to foreigners or not is a question of price. What are the resources worth to you, and what are they worth to the foreigner? If they are worth more to the foreigner than to you, it is sensible to sell them to him and use your now-enlarged capital otherwise. Fair exchange is no robbery. On the other hand, if they will in the future be worth enough more to you to compensate for the loss of return on the capital value the foreigner offers you, by all means wait. But perhaps it is asking too much to expect the peasant in us to be analytical.

Newspapers

In the New Zealand parliamentary debate, the question was raised by the Opposition why the government allowed foreigners to buy land but not newspapers. The News Media Ownership Act of 1965 was passed to prevent Lord Thompson, the native Canadian magnate from Britain, from acquiring a major newspaper. It parallels Canadian action of the same year which took the form of forbidding Canadian advertisers from deducting as business expense monies paid for advertising to non-Canadian-owned newspapers or periodicals with the exception of the Canadian editions of *Time* and *Reader's Digest*. This ruling effectively cut off attempts by American newspapers to extend their holdings into Canada. The exceptions were presumably made to obviate the charge of punitive legislation against existing companies, which were in any event widely known as foreign, with mainly foreign-source editorial material, and which had been established in Canada for the purpose of soliciting local advertising.

It is mildly ironic that Canada should be the birthplace of the world's best-known newspaper owners who conquered the press abroad, Lord Beaverbrook, now dead, and Lord Thompson, who most recently added a small group of newspapers in the Los Angeles area to his holdings. It is further true that there was no record of any attempt by American chains to acquire Canadian newspapers prior to 1965, a fact noted by the Canadian sociologist John Porter, who said this was so because Canadian newspapers were not profitable.[6]

6. John Porter, *The Vertical Mosaic* (Toronto, University of Toronto Press, 1965), p. 482.

Nonetheless, there is something to it. It is hard not to sympathize with the Canadian when he wants his newspapers owned locally, and with the southerner in the United States when he objects to the fact that the Atlanta *Constitution* and *Journal* are owned in the Middle West.

There is no objection, of course, to international trade in periodicals, such as the weekly airmail editions of *The Economist, Le Monde,* and *The Manchester Guardian,* or the nationwide sale of *The New York Times* and *The Wall Street Journal.* Clearly labeled national products can even be manufactured abroad—newspapers like the Paris edition of the New York *Herald Tribune,* the European edition of *The New York Times,* and various international editions of *Time, Newsweek, Life,* and *Reader's Digest.* Many of these cater largely to an American overseas audience plus a fringe of foreign subscribers, just as the Hilton, Pan American, and other American hotels abroad serve a largely tourist clientele from North America but also whatever local patronage they can attract. Patently American investment identified as such raises no questions. What is objectionable, it seems, is foreign control of local newspapers.

In journalism there is an inherent right of freedom of the press for anyone to say whatever he thinks, so long as it is open and aboveboard. The press can be conservative, liberal, labor, or radical, as it likes, in most countries, so long as opinion is marked as such and its origins are clear. Opinion is not a commodity to be sold to the highest bidder, although occasionally a national press will be corrupt, or subject to external influence as were French financial journals in the period before World War I. The CIA subsidy of liberal magazines enraged opinion on the right and left. The rules of the game call for everything to be clearly marked: news, opinion, and advertising; and the opinions should be those of owners who should be nationals, uninfluenced by hidden persuaders.

That there was no American attempt at penetration into the Canadian press prior to 1965—and none into any other country before or since that date as far as I know—is of some interest in the examination of the thesis that American direct investment is an instrument for world domination by the United States. Professor Porter is a Canadian sociologist in the tradition of C. Wright Mills, who wrote *The Power Elite*[7] and who believed in something approaching a conspiracy to dominate the the United States by a limited group of self-elected individuals, bound together in a communication network. In Canada, Porter says, there are three elites: the economic, the political (and bureaucratic), and the ideological. To control the country one must master all three. The ideological elite consists of three rather disparate entities: the press, educational institutions, and churches. United States interests have bought heavily into Canadian industry. They have kept their hands off the church, which in fact is dominated by bishops born and trained in Britain. In education, there was for a long time a movement of Canadian intellectuals into positions of prominence in the United States—for instance, in economics alone, Viner, Galbraith, Harry Johnson, Lloyd Reynolds, Robert Mundell, John Coleman, and a lot of others, suggesting to the credulous that Canada controls some of the power centers in the United States. In politics one has hints of pressure on the Canadian government but no evidence[8] and, conversely, hears the thought expressed

7. New York, Oxford University Press, 1956.

8. See Task Force, *Foreign Ownership and the Structure of Canadian Industry*, pp. 30, 173.

that direct investment impoverishes Canadian political life by removing from the political process a large segment of population that works for foreign industry and on that account hesitates to lobby in Ottawa in behalf of their economic interests.[9]

The newspaper issue is relatively small. Communication, transport, and finance have been called the "commanding heights" of the economy, without much analysis of what that means. I shall discuss the issue further in the section on banking. More significant is the sociopolitical issue of whether various links from the home country to the host country are separate in a market economy or additive. The Task Force comes out on both sides of this question. It mentions that the first view has some merit and is accepted by many Canadians. But then it goes on to cite Galbraith's *New Industrial State* with its technostructure.[10] The citation is not apposite. Gal-

9. Compare the boast that Atlanta is run by local interests (Coca-Cola, Lockheed, Mead Packaging, the banks and insurance companies, and so forth) whereas Birmingham depends upon a decision-making process far away in Pittsburgh. For an interesting article, which suggests that the South and West of the United States resent the East (Megalopolis) from Chicago to Boston and especially resent national corporations buying local plants, moving personnel around, and often closing down a plant after a takeover, see Daniel J. Elazar, "Megalopolis and the New Sectionalism," *The Public Interest*, No. 11 (Spring 1968), pp. 67–85. The author contrasts the new colonialism of national corporations which tended to despoil the local economies through faceless corporate managers (so that one could not blame the "robber barons") with the new sectionalism created by the federal government under the progressivism of President Lyndon B. Johnson. The affinity between the new sectionalism within the United States and nationalist resistance to direct investment abroad is exact.

10. Ibid., pp. 304–05. *The New Industrial State* was published in Boston by Houghton Mifflin in 1967.

braith's technostructure operated within the firm. There are links between firms and with the university, but this reader, at least, did not get the impression of an "Establishment" or "Power Elite," which consciously or unconsciously ran the national apparatus, and through direct investment, that of the rest of the world, in its own interest.

This is an issue which the mere economist is in no position to resolve. My instincts, or prejudices, or establishment-conditioned responses lead me to distrust the conspiracy view of society from either wing of public opinion, as alleged about the other. Rightists believe that government is infiltrated by small numbers of willful intellectuals and leftists. Many intellectuals, liberals, and radicals maintain the contrary view that government is run for industry and finance by their representatives, or at best by members of the same social class in the class interest. *The True Believer,* as Eric Hoffer calls him, in a monolithic conspiracy is certainly wrong. More than this it is difficult to establish. Are people who think alike in an unconscious conspiracy? Much depends on definitions and standards.

Banks

Foreigners are not allowed to buy further into or to start banks in Australia.[11] In Canada a recent fuss was occasioned by the purchase in 1963 by the First National City Bank of New York of the controlling interest in the Mercantile Bank of Canada, which was already owned by foreign interests of Dutch nationality and whose deposits amounted to less than 1 percent of those of all banks in

11. See "Review of Ban on Overseas Banks Urged," *The Star* (Christchurch, N.Z., June 22, 1966).

Canada.[12] In Europe the rules under which American financial institutions, ranging from banks to insurance companies, security dealers, installment loan houses, factors, express check agencies, and so forth, can establish branches, and how widely they can operate in competition with their local counterparts, cannot be readily summarized: there is a network of such institutions, operating under complex regulations, and there are difficulties in some countries—especially Germany, France, and Italy—about expanding existing institutions and establishing new or buying into domestic concerns. There has nonetheless been a substantial development in recent years, including outstanding purchases like that of the Standard Bank in London and of the Société Belge in Brussels by the Chase Manhattan Bank of New York, and that of an important interest in the Bank of London and South America, Limited, by the Mellon National Bank of Pittsburgh. United States banks operate widely in Latin America, and British in Africa, Asia, Australia, and New Zealand.

An obvious reason for keeping out foreign banks is to preserve the monopoly of local ones. German banks look with disfavor on any intrusion into the relatively tight control they have of capital markets on the one hand, and the direction of business through interlocking directorates on the other. Mr. Abs of the Deutsche Bank opposed direct investment by firms, which would be outside bank surveillance, and innovations that American security dealers sought to introduce, such as the direct sale of securities rather than sale through a bank, which

12. "Fight Emerging on Canada Bank," *New York Times* (May 16, 1966). See also Walter L. Gordon, *A Choice for Canada, Independence or Colonial Status* (Toronto, McClelland and Stewart, 1966), pp. 94–95.

holds the securities and votes them in company elections.

Conversely, the appeal by Staniforth Rocketson, chairman of the National Reliance Investment Company, Limited, for removing the ban on new overseas banks in Australia is evidently based on the desire for increased banking competition. Mr. Rocketson cited the country's need for more capital, and uncertainty about the future of the sterling bloc, which is perhaps an argument for admitting American banking interests. He stated that there is no reason why the Australian activities of foreign banks could not be subject to the same degree of control as banks already established.[13] Informed opinion will differ on this issue. On one hand, the fact that a foreign-owned bank has access to lines of credit from abroad and does not depend solely on central-bank credit locally may make it less responsive to direction from the monetary authorities. On the other hand, foreign banks are equally as vulnerable to administrative and legislation control as are domestic institutions and are usually more "visible" because of their foreign ownership. In these circumstances, the foreign-owner bank is unlikely to thwart official policy.[14]

The passive New Zealand attitude toward foreign banks, several of which are owned in London, would possibly not survive an attempt to purchase an interest in

13. "Review of Ban on Overseas Banks Urged."

14. In the annual report for 1966 of the Royal Bank of Canada, the chairman and president, W. Earle McLaughlin, characterized the argument, that foreign banks might weaken domestic monetary policies by, say, bringing in outside funds in a period when the authorities wanted to tighten credit, as "wrong." He pointed out that the Canadian authorities could control the total money supply, and that any funds brought in from the outside by foreign banks would merely reduce those available to domestic banks.

a New Zealand bank by American finance. The National
Bank of New Zealand was acquired by Lloyds Bank of
London in two stages, one representing a 40 percent interest at the end of the 1890s and the remainder more
recently, on each occasion when the bank, devoted largely
to financing butter, converted a frozen advance from
Lloyds into capital stock. The National Bank of New
Zealand has about 20 percent of New Zealand deposits.
Two banks of similar size, the Australian and New Zealand Bank and the Bank of New South Wales, are also
foreign owned, the former in Britain and the latter in
Australia. But this foreign ownership is within the family
and does not upset anyone.

The Canadian flare-up is of great interest. Walter
Gordon is the former Finance Minister in the Liberal
government, who in 1963 called for a punitive, even pro-
hibitive, tax on takeovers, tax advantages for companies
owned in Canada, government pressure to shape the
policies of foreign subsidiaries, and a government-spon-
sored Canada Development Corporation to furnish equity capital to Canadian companies to keep them out of
foreign hands. This program embarrassed the government of the day, the budget was withdrawn, and in due
course in 1965 Mr. Gordon resigned as Finance Minister.
In *A Choice for Canada* Mr. Gordon outlined the particular provisions he proposed for inclusion in the re-
vision of the Banking Law to prevent foreign penetration
into Canadian banking, limitations on the growth of the
Mercantile Bank, which was wholly foreign owned, and
restriction of any single foreign shareholder to a 10 percent interest in a Canadian bank. There is a factual dispute between Mr. Gordon and officials of the Mercantile Bank as to whether the United States interests had
bought the Dutch shareholding before or after speaking

with the Finance Minister and being informed of his displeasure. But the major legislative proposal was the consequence of his concern that another United States bank would want to enter the Canadian capital market by buying into one of the "big five" chartered banks. In the end the First National City Bank was allowed to keep its ownership of the Mercantile Bank but restricted in its capacity to expand it by a law limiting the assets of a foreign-owned bank to twenty times its authorized capital.

The American press has not left unnoticed that large Canadian banks operate branches in the United States. The Imperial Bank of Commerce is represented in a number of cities in the western United States, and the Bank of Montreal and the Royal Bank of Canada have offices in New York, Chicago, Houston, San Francisco, and some other cities.[15] But it is not hard to see that symmetry of entry is hardly appropriate between a country such as Canada, where total deposits of all chartered banks amount to less than $23 billion, and the United States, where the largest single bank (the Bank of America) had $19 billion plus in deposits at the end of 1967 and the next two largest, Chase Manhattan and First National City each, $15 billion plus.

The possibility must be considered that the five largest chartered banks in Canada, like the big four in Germany, have a monopoly they want to maintain. Higher bank charges in Canada than in the United States, however, seem to reflect less oligopolistic arrangements than lack of capital. Without being a deep student of the subject, I should have thought that the five banks in Canada were numerous enough and sufficiently active to provide effect-

15. "Fight Emerging on Canada Bank."

ive competition. The same is probably the case in Australia. Closing off banking sooner than other branches of investment is a reflection of populism, which still survives in the Congress of the United States (in the person of Representative Wright Patman)—a belief in a conspiracy of banking interests against small business and the farmer. While bankers are persuaded that theirs is a competitive industry, with some enterprises like the Ford Motor Company so large and liquid that they have no need to borrow and are able to move to other banks eager for new business if they think that any bank is slow to make credit available to them at an appropriate rate, large sections of business, trade, agriculture, and public opinion hold that banks run the economy in their selfish interest, charging exorbitant rates, having the power of decreeing life or death for other enterprises, and exercising that power ruthlessly. Banking in this view is a commanding height from which it is possible both to look deep into all aspects of the economy and to direct the flow of resources. It is a height that should be barred to the foreigner as giving him too much power.

Populism goes deep in the United States and elsewhere. In this country it has prevented banks from expanding outside their separate counties, except in a few states like California which have permitted the branch banking that applies virtually universally outside the United States. Indeed so restrictive of spatial expansion by American banks is populist sentiment inside the United States that it may force expansion abroad by blocking it at home, just as antitrust laws are believed to do in industry.

Populism and nationalism (or sectionalism) are closely related and are attitudes of the True Believer. Those who hold extreme opinions are thoroughly persuaded that the other extreme actually shapes the course of events. Nationalism can easily be carried to the point of believing that foreigners plot against the nation. Joined with populism, it fears foreign banking as the Christian Scientist fears fluoride.

There is, of course, something to the populist fear—though hardly much. There are Ponzis who swindle; J. P. Morgans who make large sums from floating stock where much of the value is represented by good will; French banks which collect peasant savings to invest in Czarist bonds while earning substantial commissions; insiders in security markets who drive up the prices of securities and sell out at the top, leaving outsiders holding the bag. "Banks are willing to lend only to those who do not need money." And so on. But the sentiment is wildly overdone.

On the whole, a casual reading of financial history would favor the view that international banking is useful in breaking up domestic banking monopoly, to the extent that the latter exists, rather than dangerous in extending monopoly from one country to another. This is not to suggest that there is a substantial degree of monopoly in Canadian banking, but if an American bank could contemplate taking a small Canadian bank and developing it aggressively, profits in Canadian banking may be above the long-run norm. Canadian monetary authorities are right in being concerned that this might start a trend in United States penetration into Canadian banks that would go beyond the point of profit maximization. If leading American banks bought out Canadian banks at uneconomic prices because of oligopolistic fear of a rival operating unpoliced in a particular preserve, they would pay Canadian shareholders more than the securities were worth and might take undue risks in an effort to justify the prices paid. But Canadian banking supervision could prevent questionable practices.

The conclusion seems inescapable that the Australian and Canadian measures against foreign banking are based on a combination of populism and nationalism, with perhaps a dash of sensible precaution against a follow-the-leader excess of entry in the Canadian case. In this they are unlike the European restrictions on financial entry which are the preservation of largely monopolistic advantages. They are equally uneconomic.

Milk Bars

Early after the war, there was an outcry in both Britain and the Dominions, especially Australia and the Union of South Africa, about a large movement of British capital abroad for investment in nonessential enterprises which were sometimes given the generic designation of "milk bars." Today Australia does not want foreign investment in soft drinks.[16] A generation ago one might have expected this about cosmetics which are a significant item of American investment in Australia and New Zealand today. Less developed countries frequently make the distinction between essential and nonessential industries and restrict foreign investors from earning profits which would have to be paid abroad in hard currency for soft drinks.

Galbraith's strictures on advertising's distortion of spending patterns from basic wants may lend support to this distinction between essential and nonessential goods, but they are not accepted by the majority of economists. All wants above a very low minimum, worth about $60 a year in 1948 when Professor Samuelson wrote the first

16. Brash, *American Investment*, p. 276.

edition of his well-known textbook *Economics: An Introductory Analysis,*[17] are socially determined. Hi-fi record players are as much the result of social influence in consumers' budgets as tail fins on Cadillacs, and the same goes for hamburgers, whole wheat bread, coffee, and similar items of consumption other than the balanced meal of soybean soup which represents minimum dietary needs. There may be psychological, sociological, and even cultural essential sets of consumption wants, but there is no such thing as a physiological minimum above the Malthusian limit, in its culture-free soybean form.

The test of what is economic cannot be put in physiological terms, but only in terms of the market. If the demand for soft drinks is sufficiently great and the cost of producing them so low that the rate of return is high, this is what, in a market economy with consumer sovereignty, is economic. If foreigners are prevented from producing them efficiently, domestic enterprise will use more resources in producing poorer products badly. The distinction between essential and nonessential goods is unacceptable, and with it the exclusion of the nonessential area of production for foreign investment.

This is an area for "second-best" analysis, however, where private values may differ from social values for one reason or another—because income distribution is inequitable but cannot be changed; because certain industries like steel, cement, and electricity have high social returns owing to external economies but low private returns, while others like alcoholic beverages may have social values below private. The economist must recognize the need for second-best policies. If soft drinks are regarded as a social waste, even though consumers spend

17. New York, McGraw-Hill, 1948.

their incomes on them, the answer is to tax them. One should tax those industries where private value is above social value, and subsidize those where the opposite is true. Such taxes and subsidies would apply to foreign and domestic entrepreneurs alike—unless the infant-industry exception to the economic rule of nondiscrimination applies. To restrict only the foreigner in those cases where exception to the rule of consumer sovereignty is appropriate—and let me make clear that I am not suggesting this is the case for soft drinks—is distortionary and uneconomic.

Foreign Investment Is Expensive

Unlike the Canadians and the New Zealanders who worry that the United States direct investment is destroying the independence of their countries, the Australian concern has been mainly that direct investment is expensive.[18] The question first arose over the General Motors-Holden accounts for 1953–54, which showed, as Mrs. Penrose pointed out, rates of return of 560 percent per annum on ordinary capital, 39 percent on shareholders' funds, 24 percent on funds employed, and 14 percent on sales, not to mention 8 percent of the total dollars earned by the Australian economy on current account in the balance of payments.[19] The numbers are impressive. They are not, however, representative. In addition, high rates of return on direct investment, when they are not economically useful in pointing the way to

18. H. W. Arndt, "Overseas Borrowing, the New Model," in H. W. Arndt and W. M. Corden, eds., *The Australian Economy* (Melbourne, F. W. Cheshire, 1963), p. 441: "Clearly American capital has been very expensive."

19. Penrose, "Foreign Investment and the Growth of the Firm," *Economic Journal, 66* (June 1956), p. 221.

shortages of products in great demand, are frequently the result of monopoly, tariff protection, or inflation, conditions over which the local governmental authorities have influence.

Data on the profitability of direct investment are spotty. The Australian figures are among the most complete, and show wide variation by countries, and a sharp decline after 1960 when import restrictions were relaxed.[20] In New Zealand, the average return of foreign investors as a whole is little above that of New Zealand-owned companies, contrary to what our theory would expect.[21] The theory is supported, however, by several considerations: United States firms have a substantially higher return than British and Australian firms, and foreign firms have a wider dispersion of profitability than their New Zealand rivals, more and higher losses,

20. See "Private Overseas Investment in Australia," in Commonwealth of Australia, *Supplement to the Treasury Information Bulletin* (May 1965), p. 19.

COMPARISON OF "EARNING RATES" OF NORTH AMERICAN, UNITED KINGDOM AND TOTAL OVERSEAS INVESTMENT IN AUSTRALIA. INCOME PAYABLE AS A PERCENTAGE OF TOTAL INVESTMENT IN AUSTRALIA

Three-year averages	From North America	From United Kingdom	From All Overseas Countries
1949–50 to 1951–52	12.6	7.9	8.9
1952–53 to 1954–55	17.7	7.2	9.5
1955–56 to 1957–58	15.6	7.7	9.7
1958–59 to 1960–61	15.4	6.8	9.2
1961–62 to 1963–64	7.9	5.7	6.4

See also Brash, *American Investment*, Chap. 10, and B. L. Johns, "Private Overseas Investment in Australia: Profitability and Motivation," *Economic Record, 43* (June 1967), 233–61.

21. Deane, "Foreign Investment in New Zealand Manufacturing," pp. 353 ff.

especially for recently established companies, and more and higher profits.[22] Canadian data on profitability are particularly sparse, but show little difference between that of foreign- and resident-owned companies. In some secondary industries, foreign-owned companies do distinctly better; there is also evidence of a falling tendency for foreign firms—from 11 to 13 percent of capital after income and withholding taxes in 1947–52 to 9 to 10 percent in 1953–57 and 5 to 8 percent in 1958–61.[23]

Systematic evidence on profits on direct investment from other sources is hard to accumulate. From 1950 to 1958, United States returns on investment in Europe (presumably book values) on an after-local-tax basis were 10.1 percent in France, 10.7 percent in Italy, 11.9 percent in Germany, 13.5 percent in Belgium, and 17.2 percent in the United Kingdom.[24] (It is an important point in support of the thesis of these lectures that the fastest-growing markets produced lower rates of return, and the slower-growing markets higher. It is not the growth of markets that gives rise to earnings, as the National Industrial Conference Board would claim, but advantages of the foreigner over local enterprise. But the demonstration is not convincing, since the faster-growing markets may have a higher proportion of new and temporarily

22. Donald T. Brash, *New Zealand's Debt Financing Capacity*, University of Canterbury Publication, No. 5 (Christchurch, 1964), p. 31.

23. See Safarian, *Foreign Ownership of Canadian Industry*, pp. 296–98; and Task Force, *Foreign Ownership and the Structure of Canadian Industry*, pp. 104–05, 219.

24. See E. A. Philipps, "American Direct Investment in West German Manufacturing Industries, 1945 to 1959," in *Current Economic Comment*, 22 (May 1960), 36, quoted by Brinley Thomas, "Recent Trends in American Investment in Western Europe," *Three Banks Review*, No. 47 (September 1960).

low-profit investment, which will reverse the proportions in the longer run.) In Norway foreign-owned enterprise has a higher share of net income of all corporations (32.4 percent) than of net worth (27.7 percent), but net income after tax was only 5.3 percent for foreign enterprise, compared with 3.3 percent for Norwegian.[25] A Reserve Bank Study in India shows that United States firms earned 13.5 and 12.8 percent after tax in 1953 and 1955 respectively, compared with 11.9 and 9.5 percent for British companies, and 6.8 and 9.4 percent for Indian firms.[26]

The data for Australia and New Zealand (and India) raise questions such as why United States investment has been more profitable than British, why the rate of return has been falling, and whether United States direct investment is in fact expensive. The greater efficiency of American firms, Brash claims, is only partly the cause of the higher return; in addition, they tend to concentrate in fast-growing and highly profitable activities.[27] This is a meaningless distinction. Efficiency encompasses the choice of outputs in great demand by the economy, as well as low ratios of inputs to outputs.

In Australia, British investments are concentrated in banking, insurance, real estate, stock and station agencies, competitive lines in which it is difficult for the outsider to have an advantage and to earn superprofits.[28] Johns argues that part of the low rate of return on British capital is owing to "defensive" investment (mentioned in the first lecture) undertaken to avoid losses. In New Zealand

---

25. Stonehill, *Foreign Ownership in Norwegian Enterprises*, pp. 124, 142.

26. Michael Kidron, *Foreign Investment in India* (London, Oxford University Press, 1965), pp. 224, 246.

27. Brash, *American Investment*, p. 30.

28. Johns, p. 260.

manufacturing, United States, British, and Australian investment is industry-specific, with high United States profits largely from vehicle assembly and pharmaceuticals in which United States investment is concentrated, as opposed to meat freezing which is the leading British-owned industry in New Zealand, and textiles and wearing apparel, which is the leading Australian-owned industry.[29] It is not irrelevant to the discussion of the previous section that profits are moderate in banking. Further, it should be noted that the British are less inclined to reinvest profits than Americans, a point that bears on the next section.

But "expensive" is meaningless unless one compares costs with benefits. Where a firm earns monopoly profits and price is above marginal cost, there is reason to object. Where, on the other hand, there is free entry and profits are high, there is a presumption that the firm is providing the public with what it wants. High profits may exist for a time until production catches up with demand. Short-run rents due to scarcity will not persist, and in the long run price will fall to long-run cost plus normal profits. This seems to have happened in the industries in which British investment is dominant, but not yet in the newer industries that have attracted American management and capital.

High profits therefore represent a monopoly rent which may be long-run and a result of restriction on entry, or transitional and a signal under free enterprise that the producer is furnishing the public something it wants. General Motors' success with the Holden lay not only in its efficient means of production and the pressure on component suppliers in Australia to adopt more effi-

29. Deane, p. 60.

cient means of production themselves, but in producing a car of the size and power that appealed to the Australian public. Mrs. Penrose points out that while profits were high, the car was sold below the market-clearing price, resulting in waiting lines of six months for deliveries. Free entry induced Ford, Chrysler, and Morris to follow where General Motors led. In this instance, where entry was free, high profits seem to have been a result of economic performance and can hardly be judged expensive in cost-benefit terms.

Australian (and Canadian and New Zealand) public opinion seems blind to the fact that high profits earned by American firms are also a function of monopoly restriction, which in turn is subject to control by host-country action. Monopolistic and oligopolistic practices are a long Australian tradition since antimonopoly measures of the Sherman Anti-Trust type were defeated early in the century. Retail price maintenance flourishes, and tariff policy is directed toward ensuring that competition from imports is held down. The tariff on automobiles was raised 10 percentage points (from 35 to 45 percent ad valorem) in August 1966 because imports from Japan had reached 7.5 percent of the total market. The Tariff Board insists on limiting competition from imports, with the result that six automobile companies produce 400,000 units a year at prices roughly double the United States level. The tariff that will keep the marginal firm going means high profits for the efficient inframarginal General Motors-Holden. Brash, Deane, and the Canadian Task Force emphasize again and again that the cost of direct investment would be reduced and its benefits increased by lower tariffs and measures against restrictive business practices.

The argument may be made that if imports were free,

most of the other producers would be squeezed out of the market and General Motors-Holden would be left as the only producer, and therefore as a monopolist. This is an unacceptable way of looking at it. Where imports are free there is competition, actual or potential, and profits will be held to competitive levels.

The decline in profits on American investments in Australia shown above in note 20 is the result partly of new entry in automobiles and oil, including especially new foreign investment, and partly of the removal of quantitative import controls in the early 1960s.[30] Australia could reduce the expense of foreign investment still further, at any time, by lowering tariffs and permitting competition from imports. Where direct investment is encouraged, and then sustained by high tariffs which are increased on occasion, it is futile to complain that profits are high.

One can argue further that the impact of General Motors-Holden dividends on the balance of payments was also the result of a failure of Australian monetary policy. In the normal course, one would expect substitution of local production for imports to improve the balance of payments: if the same number of automobiles are produced at the same price, imported components plus profits remitted must be less than the original import of finished cars by the amount of value contributed by domestic production. If the domestic price of automobiles is reduced through economies of assembly at the market, and demand has a price elasticity greater than 1, imported components and profits remitted abroad may exceed the value of previous imports of completed cars; but if national disposable income is increased by no

30. Johns, p. 244.

more than the gain in productivity, the extra amount spent on automobiles will be diverted from current imports, thereby directly improving the balance of payments, or from domestic production, which frees resources for reallocation into export or import-competing lines. Under normal circumstances, the price mechanism should keep the economy on an even balance-of-payments keel.

But if there is a big swing of demand to the Holden, and the banking system finances substantially increased installment buying of automobiles, the added expenditure increases the import of components and the rate of profits, without shifting demand and freeing resources. Is the balance-of-payments deficit a result of direct investment or of loose monetary policy? I would argue for the latter.

Too much should not be made of this last point on credit creation. The essence is that direct investment exploits monopoly advantages. In so doing, it tends to destroy them. The monopoly advantage may be created by a tariff or by restrictive business practices. The infant-industry argument for a tariff is valid, but once the investment is off and running, the tariff should be lifted.

Tariff policies, of course, serve other purposes than the regulation of the profits of direct investors. They are used to affect returns to factors and factor movements. The Task Force recognizes that Canadian "National Policy" was founded on tariffs, and Australia and Canada have used tariffs to attract both capital and labor to build their countries. The connections between protection and tariffs become complex with direct investment which is sector-specific.[31] But the Task Force fails to contemplate

31. W. M. Corden, "Protection and Foreign Investment," *Economic Record, 43* (June 1967), 209–32.

the possibility that legislating against direct investment, perhaps by lowering tariffs, may reduce the attraction of Canada for executives and other specialized personnel who have alternative employment opportunities in the United States. What cannot be accepted intellectually, though it is understandable on other grounds, is the complaint that direct investment makes excessive profits, when these profits are the result of host-country action or inaction.

Expensive for the Balance of Payments

There is still one more sense in which direct investment is said to be expensive, and this refers to the compound-interest process of reinvestment of earnings. According to the usual analysis, this is particularly expensive for the balance of payments. Company X invests a small amount in country A, perhaps with limited equity and substantial leverage through local debt. Profits are made and used for expansion. With geometric growth for a number of years, an initial investment ends up costing the country large amounts of dollars in remitted profits. "Given the compound interest process, the outflow of funds from the borrowing country can soon become quite substantial, so that it is possible for a country to be forced to borrow abroad to service its external debt."[32] The Vernon report (of the Committee of Economic Enquiry in Australia) suggests that "once an economy has a substantial body of foreign investment, it is in a sense 'on a tiger's back' unless the trade

32. Task Force, *Foreign Ownership and the Structure of Canadian Industry*, p. 251. See also ibid., p. 246: "Reinvestment of earnings raises the base on which future earnings and dividend payments arise."

balance is improving sufficiently to meet the additional income payable overseas."[33]

What both groups, and the considerable body of literature in a similar vein, especially in Latin America, fail to make clear is, first, that direct investment raises both the base from which dividends must be paid and the productive capital with which to pay them, and second, that reinvested earnings, like any other investment, are a benefit to the balance of payments when they occur as well as a drain on it in the future.

On the first point, there may be a transfer problem. But direct investment is almost always in export-increasing or import-decreasing industry, which automatically transfers the service. If it should be in home goods, the economy must reallocate some part of the new productivity into export expansion or import substitution. In fact, as the Task Force notes, there has been in actuality no balance-of-payments problem arising in Canada from direct investment, no matter how beguiling the compound-interest analysis.

But, second, the compound analysis is in error. At time t, a new direct investment is made. Its benefit to the host-country balance of payments is the capital inflow. Its cost is the present discounted value of future earnings, assuming them all remitted as dividends. These two sums at time t must be judged to be equal at the rate of profit used to discount the stream of future earnings, using the equation $C = \dfrac{I}{r}$. If the rate of profit earned by direct investment is higher than the original r contemplated by the company, this initial cost-benefit relationship for the balance of payments is changed.

33. Commonwealth of Australia, *Report of the Committee of Economic Enquiry, 1*, 283–84, para. 11.47. The entire chapter (11)

This goes back to the question of the previous section, whether direct investment is expensive, or whether, to put the point a different way, direct investment is productive. But assume that the *ex post r* is equal to the *ex ante r*. Reinvested earnings change the equality of cost and benefit at time t in no way. If one half of, say, I_{t+3} is reinvested, this produces a benefit to the host country equal to $\frac{1}{2}I_{t+3}$ and a cost of the same amount discounted at r_{t+3}. The cost of the new investment is again equal to the benefit. And the capitalized cost of remitted earnings at time t is unchanged, since added future earnings after $t+3$ are matched by a reduction in the remittances in the year $t+3$. Deane observes that "the distinction between 'new capital' and 'reinvested profits' is an artificial one," and apart from the special case of blocked profits in an inconvertible currency he is right.

Foreign Investment Restricts Exports and Produces Excess Imports

A familiar charge levied against direct investment is that the parent imposes restrictions on its subsidiaries which prevent them from exporting and lead them to over-import. The charge does not apply to resource-oriented investments, which are by and large undertaken for the sake of exports. It is directed to manufacturing investment. The accusation is on the whole muted in Europe, where, for example, American direct investment in Britain has a higher record of exporting than British firms

provides an excellent example of the ambivalence felt by mature but capital-short countries about direct investment, especially from the United States.

in the same industries. Despite this, permission is granted
to take over firms or to purchase minority holdings in
them only on the exactment of guarantees that they will
continue to push exports. In the Dominions, however,
the charge makes little if any sense.

Manufacturing industry is by and large import-
competing. If an industry is import-competing, it is an
activity in which the country has a comparative disadvantage. If it has a comparative disadvantage, it lacks
a comparative advantage, which is necessary as a condition of exporting. It is true that an industry can shift
from import-competing to exporting via the infant-
industry path, with economies of scale, external or internal, reducing costs and making it possible to sell
abroad. To a limited extent Canadian, Australian, and
even New Zealand manufacturing industries do export.
And when the Canadian, Australian, or New Zealand
subsidiary is the cheapest source of supply, it pays the
multinational corporation to use it as the source from
which to fill orders for other countries. The international
firm may be slow to recognize changes in relative costs.
In this case, the charge against direct investment carries
weight. By and large, however, the empirical investiga-
tions of Safarian, Brash, and Deane disclose that foreign
investors have not greatly restricted the serious freedoms
of their subsidiary corporations, whether or not there are
pro forma restrictions. The alternative of licensing patents or technology is likely to be equally, or even more,
restricted.

Suppose the host country wants to push exports, even
though they are not produced cheaply enough to sell on
their merits in a competitive market. Here national
policy and efficient allocation clash. Or suppose the home
country's balance-of-payments guidelines urge its domes-

tic corporations to require its subsidiaries to buy from the home country even though prices are equal or lower in the host country. Here is a similar clash. Arndt argues that overseas firms in Australia tend to buy in the home country and that this interferes with Australian policy in extending trade with Japan.[34] The facts are unclear;[35] but from an economic point of view, Australian governmental policy would probably be distortionary. There is no presumption that corporate intervention is more distortionary than governmental. If anything, the evidence points in the opposite direction, both for exports and imports.

The company faced with orders to the parent to distort the pattern of trade for balance-of-payments reasons in one direction and orders to the subsidiary to resist or to distort oppositely is in an unenviable position. Where governmental policies contradict and jurisdictions are claimed to overlap, the company is pulled in two directions. I return to this situation in the final lecture.

One point of some interest has to do with discrimination by companies. Brash is properly skeptical of the protestations of companies that they like to purchase locally, when the claim is not supported by evidence. However, he quotes L. J. Harnett of General Motors-Holden, who states that he changed the company's policy in the 1930s from buying from the head office unless local supplies were 10 percent cheaper than Detroit to buying locally unless head office prices were 10 percent cheaper.

34. H. W. Arndt, "Observations on the Prospects for Japanese-Australian Trade," *Hitotsubashi Journal of Economics, 6,* No. 2 (February 1966), 81.

35. Brash, *American Investment,* Chap. 9; Deane, *Foreign Investment in New Zealand Manufacturing,* Chap. 8; Safarian, *Foreign Ownership of Canadian Industry,* Chap. 5.

A chemical company had a 10 percent local preference rule but was contemplating changing it.[36] While the ostensible reasons given are to help the local economy or to achieve great supply flexibility through local procurement, some preference based on rule of thumb is necessary to obviate the cost of decision-making on all transactions. Small savings are not worth the cost of widespread comparison shopping. When a firm is getting started, it makes sense to rely on the parent; when it and the supporting economy have grown, however, the rule is altered, and a mild form of discrimination applied the other way.

The Contribution of Domestic Directors, Managers, and Minority Shareholders to National Independence

New Zealand has a policy of applying pressure on foreign firms to sell a portion of their equity to New Zealand capitalists. The Canadian Task Force makes the point that in most countries foreign investment policy is applied only to new applications for permission to invest and existing firms are left alone. In New Zealand, however, new bargaining takes place each time a company petitions the import control to bring in capital equipment for expansion. If the company refuses to sell shares locally, the import license may not be granted.[37]

Deane is far from persuaded of the advantages of domestic participation.

> Many of the problem areas alleged to be associated with foreign investment as distinct from local investment, can be seen to be relatively unimportant. These include, for example, the question of en-

36. Brash, *American Investment*, p. 210.
37. Deane, pp. 103–04.

couraging local share participation; concern over 'control' and 'domination' by non-residents; the employment of 'too many foreigners'.[38]

He observes the cost of increased local participation in charges for technology, possibly higher prices for purchases from the parent, fewer benefits from research, higher dividends, reduced investment, and slower growth. "The only clear advantage is as a sop to political nationalism."[39] The Canadian Task Force takes an opposite view. Canadian goals are national independence and economic growth. National independence appears in four of the five short paragraphs under "National Aims" at the outset of the Report, and comprises the last words in the Report as a whole.

> The Canadian interest is best served by ensuring that the maximum number of residents and particularly Canadian citizens be appointed to senior positions of management.[40]

> The existence of minority shareholding . . . can be expected to facilitate the decentralization of decision-making within the multinational enterprise and increase Canadian representation on boards of directors. In both respects, this facilitates the expression of private Canadian points of view through the presence of Canadian citizens as managers, directors and shareholders and may provide additional channels for the Canadian government for the exercise of its power.[41]

38. Ibid., p. 391.
39. Ibid., p. 106.
40. Task Force, *Foreign Ownership and the Structure of Canadian Industry*, p. 195.
41. Ibid., p. 344.

The foreign company, as Deane points out, wants 100 percent control to avoid conflicts of interest. The host government wants minority participation in order to create them. The Canadian Task Force would assert that conflicts already exist, and that the "Canadian presence" is necessary to ensure that Canadian interests are protected.

The issue is clearly joined, but some points can be made to bridge the differences. It is said in Australia that the only time General Motors-Holden put its foot wrong was in 1959 in buying up the minority shares of Holden in order to convert the subsidiary from a public to a private company which did not have to publish accounts. Its retreat from public notice in this way did not last long, for the Uniform Companies Act of 1961 in Australia required subsidiaries of public companies, foreign or domestic, to publish accounts as if they were themselves public companies. The Task Force in Canada recommends this sensible requirement for Canadian law.

In addition, when the United States seeks to extend its jurisdiction to subsidiaries of United States companies abroad to assist its balance of payments, to apply its antitrust law, or to tighten the net of its embargo against the Eastern bloc in strategic goods or against Cuba and Communist China in all exports, the effort should be resisted by other countries that assert jurisdiction over these companies and are pursuing different policies. In the last lecture I shall suggest that these conflicts of jurisdiction brought to bear from different vantage points on a single economic entity point up the need for harmonization of policies.

But the "local presence" is hardly a stout defense against these affronts to national independence. Deane in New Zealand and Porter in Canada point to the alacrity with which the local shareholders sell their stock when the price is right.[42]

The Canadian economist, Albert Breton, argues that national independence can be regarded as a collective capital good which a society may wish to maximize along with national income.[43] Fair enough. But surely this is a function for the state, not the individual. The state can make laws directing foreign-owned corporations and even Canadian citizens associated with foreign-owned corporations to behave in such-and-such a way, but the "Canadian presence," a cliché that spreads through the pages of the Task Force Report, is hardly likely to carry out an unexpressed Canadian purpose for the benefit of the commonweal and at a cost to the individual.

Nor is national independence costless. If the Canadian people understand the trade-offs between independence and growth or income, and choose independence, that is no one's business but their own. No doubt United States business and United States government will huff and puff. But Canada must choose. "The maximum number of Canadian citizens appointed to senior positions" in the passage quoted above presumably means the maximum number of Canadian citizens of equal training and experience to the alternative foreigners. I suspect that this number has been passed. "Constant attention

42. Deane, p. 101: "The surprising feature was the frequency with which New Zealanders actually desired to give up their total shareholding. This was especially true in a number of cases where they received what they regarded as very good offers for their shares." Cf. Porter, *The Vertical Mosaic*, p. 248: "The investing Canadian wants only to cash in. Any feelings about a share in the country's development are weakened in the case of attractive takeover bids."

43. Albert Breton, "The Economics of Nationalism," *Journal of Political Economy*, 72, No. 4 (August 1964), 376–86.

by the Canadian government is necessary if the degree of independence possible in an open economy is to be maximized."[44] Here is another constrained maximum. The way to maximize independence is to close the economy, and move to autarky. A country loses independence through trade as well as investment, through borrowing abroad in the debt form, through welcoming tourists, owning direct investments and market securities in its own turn, as well as in subscribing to the International Bank Fund, the Organization for Economic Cooperation and Development, the General Agreement on Tariffs and Trade, the International Wheat Agreement, and so forth, not to mention the network of political links to the rest of the world. To talk of national independence as an absolute, and to work to maximize it, fails to put the issues in perspective.

This homily leaves me open once again to the accusation of being an imperialist. It is useless to deny it, but I do so. In my view, a foreign antinationalist is not an imperialist.

Note well that I do not argue for 100 percent ownership, for foreign managers or foreign boards of directors. I suggest that companies and individuals should pursue their economic interests and leave to government the pursuit of the commonweal.

44. Task Force, *Foreign Ownership and the Structure of the Canadian Industry,* p. 303.

Investment in Less Developed Countries

Stimulus to Growth or Enclave?

Most of what has been said in previous lectures about direct investment in Europe and the Dominions applies as well to the less developed countries. The valid economic arguments against this form of investment—monopoly exploitation, threat to infant industries, or barrier to a second-best solution of a problem in which access to the best is unattainable—are still good. And the emotional arguments against it arising from the peasant, the populist, the mercantilist, or the nationalist which each of us harbors in his breast are equally present. But the emotion that surrounds the subject builds up, if that is possible, as one moves from the developed to the less developed setting. The gap between capacities of investor and host country is wider. This makes for differences in kind.

In developed countries, direct investment has customarily disguised itself as domestic industry. Not true of Coca-Cola or Ford, the statement applies to, say, General Motors, which produces abroad not Chevrolets or Pontiacs but Vauxhalls and Opels. In developed countries direct investment hires local labor, deals with local suppliers, recruits local management, and to a degree fades into the domestic environment. Local coloration is far more difficult to acquire in less developed countries. Production is infrequently for the domestic market, and usually for export. Varied local inputs are difficult to procure. Until the last few years, direct investment in the less developed countries took on an enclave character, in which foreign factors of production—management, capital, and frequently labor—were combined with limited host-country inputs such as a mineral deposit, tropical climate, or in some countries common labor, often organized into gangs on the comprador system. The investment linkages Hirschman suggests are stimulating to economic growth through enlarging the demand for inputs (backward linkage) or lowering the cost of outputs as inputs for other industry (forward linkage) run abroad, rather than to the host economy.[1] With little or limited economic contact with the local economy, foreign investment occupies an enclave, tightly bound to the home country, far away, but only loosely connected, except geographically, to the local scene. The issue has been analyzed in general by Singer, and studied in particular settings by Levin (Peruvian guano) and Baldwin (Rhodesian copper).[2] Even where the linkages ran necessarily to the domestic economy, as in the need for efficient farm production to feed the African miners, the stimulus brought forth response not from black natives, whose capacity to produce for the market was undeveloped, but from Europeans who moved to Rhodesia and South Africa, pushed aside the local peasants, and developed efficient large-scale farms for local miners and for export.

1. Albert O. Hirschman, *The Strategy of Economic Development* (New Haven, Yale University Press, 1958).

2. H. W. Singer, "The Distribution of the Gains Between Investing and Borrowing Countries," *American Economic Review, Papers and Proceedings, 40,* No. 2 (May 1950), 473–85; Jonathan Levin,

Bringing management, supervisory personnel, and even semiskilled labor from home meant that the foreign investor used the technology and factor proportions he was accustomed to. To be sure, where unskilled labor was available in abundance and cheap, there was an incentive to substitute it for capital. Favoring the use of the parent technology and capital/labor ratios, however, were inertia, the need to conserve scarce engineering talent, and the insistent interest of the small proportion of local labor that was hired. This often became unionized and sought high pay on the principle that the foreign investor should pay as high wages abroad as at home, regardless of the state of the labor market. There thus developed a gap in wages between the foreign enclave and the domestic sector of the economy, perpetuating two sets of factor proportions, two levels of wages, and the phenomenon known as "dual economy."

In this situation, the possibilities for misunderstanding are enormous. The foreign investor has a long list of advantages over his counterparts in the local economy—technical capacity, capital, access to markets, good management, and so on—and this enables him to exploit the local resources when local entrepreneurship is incapable

---

The Export Economies (Cambridge, Mass., Harvard University Press, 1960); and Robert E. Baldwin, *Economic Development and Export Growth: A Study of Northern Rhodesia, 1920–1960* (Los Angeles, University of California Press, 1960). Levin's study dealt with the guano industry in the second half of the nineteenth century. For a contrast 100 years later, see Michael Roemer, "The Dynamic Role of Exports in Economic Development: The Fishmeal Industry of Peru, 1956–1966" (unpublished doctoral dissertation, Cambridge, Mass., M.I.T., 1967), which studies the positive contribution to development of the latter industry.

of so doing. In short order, sections of the local economy regard themselves as ready to take a role in production and eager to share in its fruit, providing personnel and equity capital and obtaining a share of output through taxation, dividends, or in any other way. As capacity and appetite increase, not inevitably at the same pace, the host government seeks to renegotiate the initial concession. To the extent that the foreign company is reluctant to alter the terms on which it planned—a natural-enough reaction if not perhaps a wise one— government and company tend to become antagonists.

Alien in spirit, foreign investors in the past have often acted in the less developed countries as if they enjoyed extraterritorial rights, and this history of their considering themselves above the law corrupts equitable and more nearly balanced negotiation today. The humiliation of the local sovereign by formal claims to extraterritoriality in Turkey, China, and in European colonial possessions throughout the world needs no gloss. United States Marines were landed in Nicaragua and the Dominican Republic to protect the positions of American lenders. Even where the government of the investing country was prepared to respect the sovereignty of the host government, the investor himself was not always ready to. The early record is studded with cases of bribery, corruption, evasion, and like transgressions. With time this has changed, and today foreign investors protest that they are often the only law-abiding firms in some countries of fragile ethical standards, obliged to observe the letter and the spirit of the law when native firms do not, because they are visible and exposed in a xenophobic climate. As recently as 1934, however, a British company sought to smuggle out of Argentina, in cans marked "corned beef," company records which had been subpoenaed by the Senate.[3] Kidron cites a finding of the Indian Tariff Board that foreign tire companies consistently understated their profits to evade taxes as late as 1948–53.[4] The attitude of the colonizer dies slowly, and the suspicion of the colonized, with reason, more slowly.

This antagonism between host country and investing company rests not only on different production functions and factor proportions, and an unsavory historical record; in addition, their interests diverge. Both are interested in bigger pies, but for a pie of any given size, more for one means less for the other. In an interesting and important article on the Iraq Petroleum Company, Mrs. Penrose suggested that the company "exploited" the country because it received a higher return than the minimum it would have been willing to accept and still hold on to the concession.[5] This pejorative word could equally have been applied to the host country, if, as seems likely, the Iraq Petroleum Company received less as profits than the maximum it could have received without the Iraqi government's nationalizing the property. Most instances of direct investment in less developed countries are akin to bilateral monopoly, where the reserve prices of the two parties are far apart, and there is no determinate solution such as the competitive price.

3. Dudley M. Phelps, *Migration of Industry to South America* (New York, McGraw-Hill, 1936), pp. 186–87.

4. Kidron, *Foreign Investment in India*, p. 227.

5. E. T. Penrose, "Profit Sharing Between Producing Companies and Oil Countries in the Middle East," *Economic Journal, 69* (June 1959), 238–54. Mrs. Penrose concedes the force of the criticism of the text in "International Economic Relations and the Large International Firm," *New Orientations in International Relations*, ed. Peter Lyon (London, Cass, 1968). See also her book, *The Large International Firm in Developing Countries* (London, Allen and Unwin, 1968).

In this circumstance, it makes little sense to talk of exploitation. A more appropriate mode of analysis is the non-zero-sum game theory.

Non-Zero-Sum Game

A non-zero-sum game differs from zero-sum games like chess, checkers, double solitaire, and the like, where one player wins, another loses, and the sum of the scores of the two players is zero. In non-zero-sum games, the combined score of the players may end up greater than, equal to, or less than zero. Notable examples of non-zero-sum games are war, or rather its opposite, peace-keeping, marriage, raising children, attending a university. In marriage it is possible to achieve a zero result, with one partner happy, the other unhappy, and the two results exactly balanced. More usual, however, is the outcome where the couple lives happily ever afterward and the total score is positive, or the marriage fails and the total score is negative. In exactly analogous fashion, relations between an investing company and a less developed host country may be peaceful and productive, where both win, or antagonistic to the point of confiscation or withdrawal, where both lose, the company having to write off its investment and the country being left with a collection of buildings and machinery it is unable to run and the output of which it does not know how to market.

It is the thesis of this chapter that, in the bilateral monopoly, non-zero-sum game represented by direct investment in the less-developed country, there has been a steady shift in the advantages from the side of the company to that of the country. Like women who have moved from an earlier position of subservience in marriage to equality (or in some views dominance), the bargaining position of the host country has changed. Unequal partners in the beginning, when the country had every advantage in technology, management skill, capital, and markets, not to mention what I have mentioned— gunboats and Marines, and implicit or overt political power—they are today unequal partners on a different basis, with governments eager and capable of bargaining toughly with foreign companies. Long-term contracts or concessions running to 99 years are no barrier. Only in very small part is this the consequence of different cultures in which, say, a Moslem feels less than bound by Anglo-Saxon law, and in fact takes spiritual pleasure in victory over the infidel in contract negotiations. Renegotiations of contracts with long life when the underlying conditions change is familiar in the Anglo-Saxon tradition. We have renegotiation of government procurement when subsequent information reveals that profits would be exorbitant at the costs the contractor is able to achieve. A more appropriate analogy may be with the successful TV comedian whose agent has little difficulty in getting the network to tear up an old contract with years to run at $500 a week and substitute a new one at $5,000. "My client can be funny only when he's happy," the agent presumably says, "and now that he has made a hit and is worth five thousand dollars a week, he can't be happy at five hundred." Facts are more compelling than sanctity of contract. When the country overcomes the initial advantages that the company brought to the bargaining table, the call for new contracts becomes irresistible. It is even possible that the old forms are kept and the country agrees to "love, honor, and obey" when the *realpolitik* suggests otherwise.

Taking Over the Monopoly

The company starts with monopoly advantages against its customers and monopsony advantages vis-à-vis the possessors of natural resources. If the latter are lost before the former, it is entirely natural for the countries to seek not only to take over the companies' position but also to maintain the monopoly in product markets.

The advantages of the company over the host country are lost in myriad ways. The country will require the training of native labor; stipulate specified and generally rising proportions of inputs that must be procured locally; use its sovereign power to tax to impose higher levies, and its general sovereign powers to charge unfavorable foreign exchange rates; require a share of the equity capital to be sold in the local market; and so on. The more profitable the original investment, the more new entrants clamor for admission to the industry and compete for remaining concessions. The Venezuelan government auctioned off additional oil concessions in the fall of 1964 at prices that capitalized the prospective profits of the concessionaires on a 50–50 sharing basis and brought $700 million into the coffers of the Venezuelan government. Outsiders like the Italians (Mattei) and the French, Russians, and Japanese, not to mention the latecomers among the American companies, tumble over themselves to bid for new concessions in Libya, Egypt, Iraq, and elsewhere, and make it difficult if not impossible for existing companies to maintain the old relationships. In 1967 and 1968, for example, the Iraqi government informed the companies with existing concessions that it needed more income for its five-year plan and wanted the companies to propose how to provide it, either changing the sharing arrangements, expanding production, or raising prices.[6]

The outcome of the non-zero-sum game can be negative. In 1952, the Mossadegh government of Iran nationalized the Anglo-Iranian Oil Company, shutting down the plant, pushing Persian oil off the world market for a time (and encouraging a vigorous expansion of production in Kuwait). In India, in 1953, General Motors and Ford automotive companies, which had been established in the country for twenty years, closed down their operations and withdrew in the same year that new United States investments were made in oil. The automobile manufacturers insisted that they could not reasonably comply with the Indian requirements of rapidly rising proportions of local procurement of components. Little more than a decade later, the Indian government and the oil companies were mutually unhappy over a long list of problems: Soviet oil, the price of Middle East oil, the tariff on products which had been agreed at the outset, and the profits earned on refining. But where the country has not pushed so hard that it killed the golden-egg-laying goose, its share of the golden output has grown steadily at the expense of the companies. This contrasts with the Marxian view that direct investment represents neocolonialism or neo-imperialism and continues to hold formerly dependent territories in thrall despite political independence.

The oil industry provides an instructive example. Middle East production grew in World War II to such a size that a new basing point had to be established and prices could no longer be calibrated with Gulf of Mexico

6. "The Oil Squeeze," *Economist*, 226, No. 6497 (March 2, 1968), 47.

plus. Early companies in the area made substantial profits which led to renegotiation of initial concessions. In Venezuela, expanding production led to the adoption of the 50–50 agreement between companies and host governments, which was gradually extended to the Middle East. Under the formula, the sum of royalties and profits was divided 50–50 between company and host government, with profits after tax equal to taxes on profits plus royalties. The 50–50 rule had a ring of fairness and equal sharing about it. In bargaining and non-zero-sum game theory, solutions tend to come to rest on formulas that are widely familiar. Recognition obviates discussion. The companies hoped that they could hold the line at 50–50 because of its self-evident fairness—though they conceded privately that it has no validity as a market-clearing price. But more oil continued to be discovered. On the company side, new entrants brought more competition. On the country side, various producers in the Middle East and Venezuela entered into the Organization of Petroleum Exporting Countries (OPEC) which sought simultaneously to alter the basis for contracts with the companies and to maintain the prices of oil and products. New contracts with new entrants were written at 60–40, and then at 75–25, with outstanding contracts gradually modified in the direction of the terms of the new contracts at the margin. The gradualism in the late 1950s and 1960s contrasted notably with the 1952 negative outcome of the Mossadegh-Anglo-Iranian confrontation.

Note that the host countries do not object to the monopoly aspects of the oil industry. On the contrary, they object to the shift from monopoly to more competition in product markets as more and more entrants come into the industry. Nor do they want perfect competition in factor markets. Here the goal is a shift from monopsony on the part of the companies to monopsony on the part of the host countries.

In goods markets, the monopoly is not to be destroyed; it is to be taken over. The non-zero-sum game shifts from war between two participants into collusion against third parties. By taxing the companies on the basis of posted rather than discounted prices at which oil is actually sold, OPEC helps to cut back production and to hold up price.

There are other interesting aspects of this game, which threatens to spill over the confines of the original arena. The Saudi Arabian government (SAG) puts forward the interesting claim that it is entitled to a share of profits on oil of Saudi origin at all subsequent stages of production and distribution after it has left SAG jurisdiction on its way to automobile tanks and furnaces all over the world. The legal question as to the basis on which SAG is entitled to levy taxes on productive activities outside its jurisdiction is critical, but need not detain the economist. He is interested to observe that when bargaining power has shifted sufficiently in favor of the host country, no holds seem barred. Moreover, SAG is putting pressure on the Arabian American Oil Company (Aramco) to move its head office from New York to Dhahran, where its activities will be more exposed. The company resists and delays, but with limited bargaining strength in this sort of game, refuses flatly with the greatest reluctance.

The consequences of refusal are well illustrated by the Indian, Ceylonese, and Cuban requests to various international oil companies to process Russian crude oil in their refineries. The basis of the request, of course, was that Soviet oil was cheaper than Western production, not only in cents per barrel but also in scarce foreign exchange. Western oil costs convertible dollars; Soviet oil is marketed under credit arrangements, and in barter agreements against commodities produced in the less developed countries. It would seem a normal exercise of sovereignty to discriminate against one source of imports in favor of another in the interest of conserving foreign exchange, especially in favor of a cheaper as against a more expensive product. But the oil companies are not without bargaining power. Their profits are made from the sale of crude oil, which is subsidized by a depletion allowance under United States taxation, not from refining. To ask them to refine oil that they have not produced is to ask them to operate without profits. Moreover, there are technical difficulties in converting a refinery adjusted to one sort of crude petroleum to process another with different boiling point, wax content, sulphur, and so forth. When one does not want to do something, it is usually possible to find technical reasons why one cannot. In India, the companies got away with it, in the sense that they went on refining their own crude—though at a heavy long-run cost in good will. In Ceylon and in Cuba, the local governments nationalized the oil companies. The United States government was obliged by Congress to halt foreign aid in the Ceylonese case; in Cuba the breakdown of diplomatic relations led to blockade and worse. The action of the international companies in refusing to process the Soviet oil may have been technologically justified. In Cuba, too, the companies may have written off their investments when Castro came to power so that the refusal to lose money was economically justified. In most countries, however, the rule of thumb is to string along, through thin and thinner, in the hope of an ultimately brighter outcome.

The oligopolistic feature of direct investment with its divergent interests and shifting alliances is nowhere better illustrated than in the infighting among Arab League countries over the division of the spoils, or profits, from the Trans-Arabian Pipeline (Tapline) which crosses a thousand miles of Saudi Arabia, small bits of Iraq and Syria, and emerges on the Mediterranean in Lebanon. There was first the question of how much to charge for the transport of oil: the opportunity cost of taking oil through the Red Sea and Suez Canal, which would give a big return on Tapline's investment, or the public-utility rule of cost plus a normal profit, which would create two prices for oil in the Eastern Mediterranean—cheap pipeline oil and more expensive oil fetched by tanker—and give rise to a problem of allocation.

Leaving aside this riddle, the answer to which determined the amount of profit to be taxed, regard for a moment how taxes on these profits should be divided by country. Saudi Arabia had one answer: per mile. Lebanon, with the outlet, regarded the intake and outlet as the most productive contributions to transport, and asserted that it and Saudi Arabia should divide the lion's share of the profits. Iraq and Syria, of course, considered that the essence of the contribution of a country to pipeline transportation was that sovereignty was violated. Tapline violated the sovereignty of four countries; taxes on its profits should be divided equally among them. To an economist, the sad thing is that there is no basis in this sort of bilateral monopoly situation for saying that one view is more nearly right than another. An economic question degenerates, or perhaps one should say is converted, into a political one.

There is a temptation on the part of many well-meaning persons to suggest that the direct investing company should bargain gently and generously, offering to-day to do things that the country might not think to ask for until tomorrow. Build roads, railroads, schools. Develop local suppliers in advance of the country's drive for "indigenization" (appalling coinage).[7] Train local labor and higher senior personnel from the cadres of native white-collar employees.[8] Perhaps. But the bargaining process is unpredictable. A cooperative attitude exhibited by the company may elicit cooperation or it may lead the host country to increase its demands. If it works, it was cooperation. If it fails, it turns out to have been appeasement.

A way out of the dilemma posed by these tactical questions is often sought in the adoption of rules. A country announces guidelines for foreign investment, or a basic investment law, which presumably commits it in advance to behave uniformly toward all foreign investors. But the postwar record suggests that this device is of limited help. When big and important companies threaten to get away, exceptions are made, and if too many average-size investments escape, rules are changed. Games subject to frequent rule changes are exasperating to young and old alike. There is always the temptation to think that another standard of conduct for investors and set of rules for host countries could settle the matter for at least a few years. Enough clever people have failed in the attempt, however, to lead to the conclusion that the bilateral monopoly problem with no determinate solu-

7. For an account of the Iraq Petroleum Corporation's attempts to develop local suppliers in Iraq, see Kathleen M. Langley, *The Industrialization of Iraq* (Cambridge, Mass., Harvard Middle Eastern Monographs, No. 5, 1961).

8. G. M. Meier suggests that a fair requirement for the less developed countries to impose on investing companies is that one-quarter of the senior personnel of a country should be native within five years *(Leading Issues in Economic Development* [New York, Oxford University Press, 1964], p. 163).

tion, and with shifting bargaining strength, does not lend itself to the rule of law. It remains a highly political as well as economic process.

The Acquisition Price

In non-zero-sum games, the history of the play may take on great importance, especially when the players become antagonists rather than cooperators. This point has been made in connection with oil concessions, and colonial or neocolonial relationships. It arises in still another connection: when foreign investors buy virtually bankrupt firms.

The purchase of bankrupt firms as a basis for a foreign investment does not always cause concern. Stonehill says factually that many foreign takeovers in Norway were in lieu of bankruptcy or major reorganization.[9] Deane lists ten companies in New Zealand that were taken over by foreign investors when they were losing money and discusses especially two, Enzlon Chemical Fibres and the McKenrick Glass works, which were rescued by foreign investors after failing despite government subsidy.[10] In these takeovers, the foreign investor seems to be regarded with equanimity or approval when he buys into a failing company and saves jobs (or some of them), output, national income, and so on.

Not so in at least some less developed countries. Writing to *The New York Times* from Brazil, Professor Robert J. Alexander, in February 1966, excoriated foreign, particularly American, firms for buying existing companies—an attack on takeovers as opposed to new

9. Stonehill, *Foreign Ownership in Norwegian Enterprises*, p. 99.
10. Deane, "Foreign Investment in New Zealand Manufacturing," pp. 121, 137, 356.

productive investment—and especially for "taking advantage of a weak moment in the Brazilian economy to
obtain at relatively low prices enterprises which have
been built up by Brazilians."[11] Ten months later, the
same newspaper carried an account of speeches opposing
the anti-inflation policies of the Castelo Branco government in Brazil, which were leading to the "denation-
alization" of the Brazilian economy, since American
companies can survive with foreign backing while domestic companies go under.[12] A particularly interesting
case is presented by the pharmaceutical plant that Abbott
Laboratories was about to buy control of in Ghana for
a fraction of the price which the Nkrumah government
had paid for it. So sharp was the Ghanaian outcry over
the price that Abbott Laboratories gave up the project,
and the factory remains idle.[13]

The issue is a tricky one. Alexander's distinction between takeovers and productive investment, which is
echoed in many foreign criticisms, was analyzed in the
third lecture and rejected. Moreover, if a firm fails be-

11. Letter to *The New York Times* (February 15, 1966).

12. "U.S. Investment Scored in Brazil," *New York Times* (December 18, 1966). It should be noted, however, that substantial imports
of print cloth from Brazil to the United States took place in 1965
at the instance of the U.S. Department of State, which urged im-
porters to buy exceptional amounts of cloth to help counteract
the deflation which left Brazilian mills with sizable inventories and
a shortage of foreign exchange. James Thornblade, "Textile Imports from Less-Developed Countries and the Competitive Challenge to the American Textile Industry" (unpublished doctoral
dissertation, Cambridge, Mass., M.I.T., 1968), Chap. 5.

13. "Ghana State Enterprises: Abbott Agreement Criticized,"
West Africa, No. 2634 (November 25, 1967), p. 1527. See also
"Ghana's Economic Hopes Bright," *New York Times* (March 4,
1968).

cause of inefficiency or technical incapacity, as in Enzlon and the McKenrick Glass company in New Zealand, foreign investment helps rather than hurts. Bygones are bygones in economics, if perhaps not in all fields; if the assets sell for what they are worth, the seller should be satisfied. In the last century there was a saying in Grenoble, a city of notoriously euphoric investors, that a hotel was a good investment after the second bankruptcy. No one blamed the third owner for waiting.

But these considerations do not dispose of the problem. Two aspects raise difficulties: the first relating to anti-inflation policies, imposed on a less developed country by international agencies such as the International Monetary Fund (I.M.F.); the second, to the waste of assets by government, which makes the price at which they are sold to foreigners a political or, at least, a public issue.

The Brazilian economy has adapted itself for years to continuous inflation. To the extent that this is distortionary, a halt imposed from abroad changes the assumptions that went into many investment decisions and alters the value of the assets. If foreign interests impose the deflation and other foreign interests take advantage of it, it is easy to understand ensuing national frustration and anger. In 1945 in these circumstances, the United States imposed a moratorium on new acquisitions in Germany. Alexander's view that businessmen ought to hold back from buying undervalued properties suggests either a lack of interest in maximizing profits or a horizon over which they are maximized so long in time as to make profit-maximization meaningless. In a period of deflation, or of stability after inflation which becomes relative deflation, the individual seller who disposes of his property is better off, as revealed by his preferences. If government chooses to prevent sales to foreigners at such a time, it is certainly understandable.

The Abbott-Ghana case seems to have turned entirely on price. Under Nkrumah, Ghana had bought a number of "turn-key" plants which proved incapable of covering their capital and operating costs and yielding a normal profit. Completed plants, they needed management capable of operating them. The new Ghanaian government stated it had to sell control of the pharmaceutical plant built on a turn-key basis by the Hungarian government because "we needed a know-how partner." Abbott Laboratories seems to have bargained hard, acquiring 45 percent of the shares and management control for 1 million cedis (equal after the devaluation of July 1967 to about $1 each), and with them exclusive contracts to supply government hospitals, agencies, and the armed forces. The only issues seem to have been the price and perhaps the exclusive arrangements. Firestone Rubber Company acquired 45 percent of the equity of Ghana Rubber Estates and 60 percent of that of Firestone-Ghana, which makes tires and rubber goods, for $2.35 million, which caused no excitement, and Pan American Airways acquired two hotels.[14] But price is important when the outcome of the negotiations is a public concern. Whether Abbott Laboratories or the Ghanaian government was at fault cannot be judged from a distance, although the Ghanaian ambassador to the United States is not disposed to blame the company. In bilateral monopoly bargaining in public, it may be that no outcome satisfactory to the company will be acceptable to the body politic.

14. *West Africa*, No. 2612 (June 24, 1967), p. 825.

Restricted Industries

In the developed countries, including Europe, Japan, and the Dominions, foreign investment is prohibited or restricted in a number of industries—natural resources, banking, transport, communications, soft drinks. Less developed countries are also inhibited in these areas. Focusing attention on economic development, however, they object as well to other activities. The point can be made by reference to a set of criteria for foreign investment issued by India in the 1950s. Foreign investment would be welcomed where

1. there was a genuine program of manufacturing;
2. it took place in a field where domestic investment was inadequate;
3. the activity was export-increasing or import-decreasing;
4. it increased productivity;
5. the foreign company trained native personnel;
6. domestic capital was admitted into the company at all stages.

In 1964 the point about the balance of payments and productivity was put more simply if not more understandably. The doors were opened still wider to foreign investments "as long as the burden of such investment on the balance of payments in future is not disproportionate to its contribution to our economic growth."[15]

15. *Indian News* (Washington, D.C., February 15, 1964). See also the advertisement by the Venezuelan government in *The New York Times* (January 22, 1968), in which Dr. Hector Hurtado, economic adviser to the Venezuelan government said that his country is selective in welcoming foreign investment and "discourages the dispersion of capital into nonessential activities that stand in the way of industrial integration."

The training of labor and the admission of domestic capital into foreign investment have been discussed. It remains to analyze the contribution of foreign investment to growth in terms of manufacturing, the adequacy of local investment in an industry, the contribution to productivity, and the cost to the balance of payments.

Most interesting are the requirements that investment be in manufacturing and in lines in which domestic investment is inadequate. To the economist this point looks again like the fallacy of misplaced concreteness. There may be reasons to exclude foreign investment in certain activities—reasons, as previously noted, of defense, monopoly, infant-industry, or second-best character. But the notion that manufacturing contributes more to growth than agriculture or services is both widespread —services are not even part of national income in Soviet macroeconomic accounting—and subversive of the development process. Along with misplaced concreteness, there may also be a dash of the *post hoc ergo propter hoc* fallacy. The first edition of Colin Clark's *The Conditions of Economic Progress*[16] observed that the more developed a country was, the greater the proportion of its resources engaged in secondary activities like manufacturing, mining, and construction, and the smaller that employed in primary agriculture, fishing, and forestry. The lay observer concluded that the path to economic development lay through manufacturing. The economist, on the other hand, is persuaded that resources of capital, land, and labor should be employed where they can earn the highest return without regard to the physical character of the activity. If higher returns can be earned in agriculture or distribution than in manufacturing,

16. London, Macmillan, 1940.

and investment has been carried far enough to produce diminishing returns and lower profits, it is time to divert savings into the next most profitable occupation. This indirect route leads to manufacturing where the direct path through building manufacturing facilities when they are not the most profitable investment outlet will not. To forbid entry into agriculture or services if returns are high in those activities and attract the foreign investor is to perpetuate local monopolies and to slow down growth.

The argument is made that manufacturing provides external economies in bringing labor to the city from the village, liberating society from the extended family system, providing specific skills, and so on. There is something to the argument as applied to agriculture, but it can be exaggerated in the case of retail distribution. Commerce is a school for industry. It is no secret that commerce trains entrepreneurs how to keep books and to maximize, and further assists the accumulation of capital. Not by accident did the Commercial Revolution of the Middle Ages precede the Industrial Revolution. Less developed countries today associate development with dams, transmission towers, chemical complexes, and factories rather than with offices, stores, warehouses, hotels. The United States government does not succumb to this fallacy. In proposing guarantees as a stimulus to foreign investment in less developed countries limited to industries "most closely related to economic development and involving the greatest risk," it specified

> manufacturing, retailing, processing or marketing of agricultural products, ownership or operation of hotels, fishing, and certain service industries, and under limited conditions, wholesaling and construction. Among the excluded industries are extraction

of minerals, refining, shipping, banking, communications and insurance.[17]

The exclusions seem based primarily on the level of risk,
presumed to be low in mining, refining, shipping, and
banking, though perhaps not in communications and
insurance. Manufacturing does lead the list, to be sure.
But the point is well made that retailing, marketing, and
(under limited conditions?) wholesaling are closely related to economic development, despite the Indian view
to the contrary. The same could be said of undramatic
storage facilities.

Restriction of foreigners in retail trade may be based
on the infant-industry argument. In many parts of Asia
where Chinese or Indian merchants had established roots
in retail marketing, new entry has been forbidden and
old entrants have been pushed out, in an effort to enable
native workers to gain employment in distribution and
obtain the training it affords. An act of 1954 in the
Philippines provided that by 1964 no foreigner could
be engaged in retail trade. (Under the parity legislation that accompanied Philippine independence, this
act did not apply to United States citizens, who must
be treated on a par with Filipinos until 1974.) The 1954
act is understandable in terms of the infant-industry
exception to the rule that investment should be allowed
in those occupations in which investors think they can
make money. But regulation of this sort may quickly
lead from learning by doing to monopoly, and Filipino

17. U.S. Congress, Committee on Foreign Affairs, *Foreign Assistance Act of 1964, Hearings*, 88th Congress, 2d Sess. (Washington,
D.C., G.P.O., 1964), Part 1, p. 46, quoted by Marina von Neumann
Whitman, *Government Risk-Sharing in Foreign Investment* (Princeton, Princeton University Press, 1965), p. 52 n.

businessmen have not been slow to exploit the opportunities. A Philippine treasury interpretation in April
1963 stated that an oil company that was 98 percent but
not 100 percent American-owned was not a United States
citizen, and hence ineligible to market its products at the
retail level in competition with Filipinos. Vertical integration thus becomes impossible in an industry where it
offers positive advantages. Subsequent rulings laid down
that selling by one company to another company is retail trade, and hence a monopoly of Philippine (and 100
percent United States) business. On this basis, each foreign investor, and after 1974 each United States investor,
will have to acquire a Filipino associate to sell his product.[18] It seems likely that many companies will quit because of this need to share their real or monopoly advantage with a monopolist.

To forbid foreign capital to enter industries where
domestic investment is already adequate is another rule
that sounds reasonable. In the Philippines, the nationalist as opposed to the development school on foreign
investment wants foreign capital "to supplement, but not
to supplant" local enterprise. But these slogans have no
meaning in economic analysis. The United States petroleum industry has long talked of imports to supplement
but not supplant domestic production, a concept which
makes sense only if supply and demand curves are completely inelastic with respect to price. If the United States
were to produce 9 million barrels of oil a day and consume 11 million barrels a day, both regardless of price
within a reasonable range, then 2 million barrels of oil
per day imported to supplement (but not supplant)
domestic production would make sense. Where demand

18. Seminar paper of Felipe Suva Martin (Cambridge, Mass.,
M.I.T., April 26, 1967).

and supply respond to changes in price, however, the slogan is empty. Each barrel imported both supplants higher priced oil and supplements production of equal or lower cost. Any limitation of imports, moreover, frustrates demand which would have been met at a lower price. In the same way the adequacy of domestic industry in a country is determined only by its profitability. If an industry earns greater than normal profits so that it is attractive to foreign capital, there is a presumption that the domestic capital engaged in it is less than "adequate." Competition from abroad will supplement the low-cost producers in the industry, and supplant the high-cost.

The Indian attitude on these questions is not held with rigid consistency. In 1954 there was an outcry and a call for a return to the Swadeshi movement (which had boycotted British industry in 1905–08) because a foreigner had been allowed to enter the production of ink, a product the Indian public thought competently handled by Indian producers. An official report of a year later, on the other hand, welcomed foreign capital in industries like textiles, cement, and paper, where India had already established herself. For the most part, however, preference is given to foreign enterprise entering heavy chemicals, pharmaceuticals, synthetic oil, heavy machinery, iron and steel, and aircraft production—manufacturing industries of technical complexity and managerial difficulty.[19] To the extent that these are import-competing and require tariffs, the question is whether India should produce them at all rather than buy on world markets and import them. Fewer Indian resources may be required to import than to produce these items inefficiently

19. Kidron, *Foreign Investment in India*, pp. 109–10, 155. For a discussion of the Swadeshi movement, see ibid., p. 25.

at home. It is by no means certain that India lost in economic development when General Motors and Ford withdrew their investments from that country in 1953. It is clear that development in Argentina and Brazil, on the other hand, has been slowed down by maintaining heavy protection for automobile manufacturing and encouraging numbers of foreign producers to produce domestically at inefficient scales of output.

Balance-of-Payments Considerations

The balance-of-payments aspects of direct investment in less developed countries are no different analytically than in Europe or the Dominions, but conditions are slightly altered, and some new arguments have been added. An altered condition is implied by the Indian requirement that foreign investment be export-increasing or import-decreasing. In a modern economy capable of reallocating resources among sectors to meet balance-of-payments needs, such a requirement would be based on the partial-equilibrium fallacy. Here is a new investment which has to take care of itself with nothing else changed. If nothing else can change, investment in home industry will worsen the balance of payments, as the extra income generated spills over into imports and the dividends earned by its foreign owners are presented for transfer into foreign exchange. In these circumstances, investment from abroad must provide for the transfer of profits on its own, and hence be limited to exports or import-competing industry.

Partial-equilibrium analysis does not apply in an economy that is responsive to market signals. Capital should be invested in the most profitable line in the economy, and the transfer of dividends should be handled through the economy's macroeconomic apparatus. If the investment is export-increasing or import-decreasing, transfer of dividends may be assumed to take care of itself. But if investment takes place in the domestic sector, transfer is still possible. Sale of its output diverts purchasing power from other types of expenditure. Some may be drawn directly from imports, thus helping the balance of payments at the second stage, or from exportable goods which will be sold abroad now that their market has declined at home. The diversion of purchasing power from home production frees resources which can move into exports or into import-competing production. Should this not take place automatically, measures to assist the process along may be required: monetary or fiscal contraction, currency depreciation, incomes policy to hold down wages while they rise abroad, or some such macroeconomic instruments. By assumption, direct investment in the domestic sector is the most productive possible investment. To capture a portion of that productivity to make good on debt service is a relatively simple matter for an economy that is capable of transformation.

But a less developed economy may be incapable of transformation whether because the economy gives the wrong price and income signals or because consumers and producers fail to respond to correct signals. In this case there may be a second-best argument for requiring each investment to provide for transfer of its own dividend income. This is a weakness of the economy, not of direct investment. (Parenthetically, the United States is currently behaving like an underdeveloped country in requiring separate companies and projects to calculate the direct balance-of-payments effect of their business projects. In a well-functioning economy, the balance of payments is a matter for macroeconomic policy, not case-by-case intervention.)

The trade-off between contribution to economic growth and balance-of-payments burden suggested by the *Indian News* is a dilution of the requirement that each investment provide for transfer of service on its own debt. But it is hardly operational. Contribution to growth is proportional to profitability when there is no monopoly and when there are no external economies or diseconomies, including training effects, linkages, and so on. If these exist in less developed economies, contribution to growth must be measured by profitability of various investments using shadow prices that reflect development demands and scarcities. This takes us back to deciding which industries are open to foreign investors and which closed. We are back, too, at the temptation to argue that manufacture is productive and distribution is not.

A balance-of-payments point touched on in connection with Canada perhaps deserves another word. It is the Latin American tendency to compare debt service on outstanding investment with new capital inflows. When new investment falls below current debt service, the Latins claim that foreign investors are taking more out of Latin America than they are putting in. Implicitly they would approve of continuous reinvestment of dividends, a pyramiding technique to which Australia and Mrs. Penrose object. Their concern is that the merchandise import surplus which transfers this year's capital imports must be altered into an export surplus next year to transfer the interest and dividends on last year's capital. If new loans are made, this pressure on the balance of payments is avoided.

This reasoning is totally unacceptable. Collado and Bennett make a formal point against one way of quantifying the charge. They hold that it is unfair to compare the net new investment of a company with remitted interest and dividends, rather than gross investment with interest, dividends, and amortization.[20] If Creole Petroleum in Venezuela takes $100 million of dividends in a given year and adds only $50 million to its investment, net, one should not compare the $100 million out with the $50 million in but should add, say, another $100 million of amortization to both sides. This would make the comparison $200 million taken out and $150 million put back in and greatly improve the ratio. Since amortization was earned in dollars, it could have been taken out; its reinvestment therefore was an act of volition, akin to new net investment. To a highly rational company like the Standard Oil Company of New Jersey, which owns Creole and for which Collado and Bennett worked, it is logical to deal with total cash flow, including profits and amortization, rather than merely profits. A high level of rationality requires a company notionally to run down all of its investments all over the world and to take positive decisions to build them back to their previous level, or to expand them. Most companies, however, operate by the rule of thumb that an investment should survive from year to year and automatically maintain it by reinvesting amortization unless events positively call for a decision to let it run down. There is something, then, to the point about what quantities should be compared, though not a great deal.

But Collado and Bennett give away too much when they concede, as we do not, that it is appropriate to compare interest and dividends remitted from a country with the inflow of new investment to the country. The two sums have nothing to do with one another except in a

20. E. G. Collado and J. F. Bennett, "Private Investment and Economic Development," *Foreign Affairs, 35* (July 1957), 631–45.

narrow balance-of-payments context. When loans are for consumption, which is at a minimum level, it is true that next year's borrowing must provide for interest on this year's outstanding loans. As experience with loan sharks indicates, moreover, to borrow once is to commit a country to borrow annually on a rising compound-interest scale.

But this analysis is irrelevant to productive investment. Each loan provides an increase in total productivity from which debt service can be paid. No borrowing is needed to pay debt service, since debt service is earned by the investment projects associated with past loans. There is no need for foreign investors to reinvest their earnings, or for any single original investment to grow geometrically. The Latino comparison makes sense only where past investment has been used unproductively, or where the productivity has not been accompanied by the appropriate reallocation of resources to produce the exports or economize on imports sufficiently to produce the foreign exchange needed for debt service. This may well be the case—though not, to be sure, in investments in Venezuelan oil. If it is true, the fault lies elsewhere than in the unwillingness of foreign investors to relend their interest and dividends.

On the implicit model behind the Latin American view, any initial investment must be pyramided ad infinitum. It is impossible to make a single productive investment and enjoy its income. Lenders must relend interest and dividends, and borrowers must go on borrowing at a growing level.

The Short Run and the Long

In a liberal competitive system, firms lack power and countries do not intervene. There is a determinate solution. Resources are allocated by the invisible hand—price. Firms maximize profits, and, in the absence of monopoly, scale economies (including the infant-industry case), and the need to turn to the second-best, maximize national income as well.

Direct investment is otherwise. Firms have power over price, and governments intervene. But firms and governments have an opportunity to choose the basis for intervention and, specifically, whether they are concerned with short-run or long-run interests. The difficulties crowd in especially where firm and country, engaged in confrontation, choose different standards of conduct or wear each other down with countervailing power.

Take the interest of the firm: in the short run it benefits from paying the lowest possible prices for inputs and getting the highest possible return for outputs. Under competition, it pays competitive prices for factors and sells goods at competitive prices. In monopolistic competition it benefits from buying at monopsonistic prices and selling at monopoly prices—in the short run. But short-run maximization may breed ill will and encourage entry. An important judgment is how long these reactions will take to be realized, and at what rate of interest one should discount the difference between monopoly profits and some lower level that produced a lesser reaction. The company with a low rate of interest may maximize its life expectancy, if not its short-run profits, by charging prices below the monopoly and, approaching the competitive level, by paying somewhat more than monopsony wages, rents, royalties, and taxes, to the extent that it can affect its taxes by choosing where to earn income. It may buy supplies locally in the host country despite their higher price, or it may import supplies from the parent despite *their* higher price, depending upon which government it chooses to court more assiduously. Still a longer-run view may be to calculate competitive prices and buy and sell where profits would be maximized on this basis. The procedure can be defended by liberal standards. In the late 1920s and early 1930s there was a musical-comedian named Joe Cook whose best known act was the imitation of seven Hawaiians. By the same token, it is possible for a monopoly-monopsony, or a large company with great advantages over the competition in buying inputs and selling outputs, to act as if it operated in competitive markets.

For the host country, short-run maximization conduct turns on whether it wants to attract another company as an investor. If so, it must behave generously toward direct investors. If not, the maximization course in the very shortest run probably lies through confiscation. Martin Bronfenbrenner commented on the point more than ten years ago in a classic article,[21] an article which is as up-to-date as today's newspaper as one contemplates, for example, the action of Tanzania in seizing foreign-owned banks and flour mills entirely, and taking substantial interests of 60 or 50 percent in other foreign investments, including a new cement plant which had been operating less than a week.[22] The Canadian Task Force observes that countries tend to pay too much attention to new investment and too little to established enterprises. Certainly, as successive new investments enter a country, the importance of the inframarginal units grows and

21. Martin Bronfenbrenner, "The Appeal of Confiscation in Economic Development," *Economic Development and Cultural Change,* 3 (April 1955), 201–18.

22. "Tanzania Seizes More Businesses," *New York Times* (February 11, 1967).

that of the marginal unit relatively declines—in the short run. If, however, the host country takes a longer view and wishes to attract a flow of new investment rather than one company at a time, the appeal of confiscation goes down. Three months after his wave of confiscation in Tanzania, President Julius K. Nyerere called for new private United States investment on a 50–50 basis.[23] To reverse Keynes' aphorism, the short run extends into the long.

Short-run policy by the host country can err in the opposite direction and try too hard to seduce the foreign investor. United States companies' ten-year freedom from corporate income tax in Puerto Rico is one example, but there are many more.[24] Jagdish Bhagwati is concerned with "unhealthy competition of underdeveloped countries to attract private foreign investment" and seeks "a common code which would coordinate and match the various advantages they hold out to various prospective investors."[25] But, of course, there will always be a

23. "Nyerere Appeals to U.S. Investors," *New York Times* (May 25, 1967).

24. See, for example, the special fiscal benefits set forth in "Privileges to Investors," an advertisement of the Banco de Guatemala, *New York Times* (January 22, 1968); "Investment in Thailand," an advertisement in a special Thailand supplement to *The New York Times* (February 28, 1962); "Indonesia Eases Investment Law," *New York Times* (December 26, 1966); and "Make It Ghana, Please," *Economist*, *220*, No. 6415 (August 1966), p. 563. This last article observes that Ghana is in the same boat as Britain: "It is very difficult, in the short run, to woo foreign money and a domestic electorate simultaneously."

25. Jagdish Bhagwati, *The Economics of Underdeveloped Countries* (New York, McGraw-Hill, World University Library, 1966), p. 223. Another suggestion is for the establishment of an Andean Development Corporation to negotiate with foreign investors on behalf of the Andean group of countries on the west coast of Latin

temptation for the poorest countries, or those that have accumulated an unproductive debt, to chisel. United States lack of interest in tax-sparing, as mentioned earlier, is designed to limit this erosion of the tax base of the less developed countries for the long-run benefit of all.

Finally, the country of the parent company. In the short run, work hard in the interests of the investing company, including the use of force, reprisal, naked diplomatic pressure, and so on. In the long run, relax. Some progress from the short toward the long run has been made in the self-image of the investing countries, but it gains little credibility abroad from those who think that big and strong governments push around the little and weak for immediate economic advantage. Perhaps we are too close to these matters to acquire perspective.

To return for a moment to game theory. If countries and companies were to operate on long-run principles of cooperation and even dealing, the outcome would be positive gains on both sides. But either company or host country may be greedy or necessitous and move to short-run maximization. When both maximize in the short run, the outcome is indeterminate, save for the antagonism. One short, the other long is more nearly determinate—the maximizer wins over the cooperator—but the game is likely to run down. The difficulty remains— how to get it going again on a mutual long-run basis. How does one party make peace when the other wants war?

America, and especially to attract investors into the "dynamic" industries while preventing tariff competition to attract them into "vegetative" industries. See Carlos F. Diaz-Alejandro, "The Andean Group in the Integration Process of Latin America," paper submitted to the Conference on the Economic Integration of Latin America, May 9–11, 1968, Stanford, California.

Disaggregated Interests

Previous lectures have indicated that the national interest is a weighted sum of separate sectional interests which do not by any means converge. We take this as read, and forbear to grind through the permutations and combinations. One interesting point to bear in mind, however, is that local entrepreneurship may work with foreign enterprise in symbiosis, or be counterpoised and ready to inherit its position of wealth and authority. The nihilist position of Franz Fanon is opposed to both. In a world too sordid and corrupt to be worth saving, it is necessary to destroy foreign investment in the interest of a brighter future, based on not-yet-specified plans and institutions. But since domestic entrepreneurship, too, is rotten to the core, it must not be allowed to take over.[26] The apocalyptic notions of Fanon are perhaps not widely shared by the nationalists in the less developed countries, save for the Maoists. Host country and company, however, may find themselves so intent on winning their own game, whether separately or together, that they miss the figures working toward them to kick over the board and break it up for both.

26. Franz Fanon, *The Wretched of the Earth* (New York, Grove Press, 1965).

The International Corporation

National, Multinational, or International?

While the large firm with worldwide interests has been called many things in its day—not all complimentary—usage is beginning to settle on three major terms, with fixed distinctions among them. These are the national firm with foreign operations, the multinational corporation, and the international corporation.[1]

1. See Task Force, *Foreign Ownership and the Structure of Canadian Industry*, p. 33, where the connotations given to the definitions are slightly pejorative: the first is a national corporation, operating extranationally, "insisting on the primacy of the methods it uses at home, and even of the laws of the home country." The second is "a multinational corporation in a genuine sense, sensitive to local traditions and respecting local jurisdictions and policies." The third is "global, with such pervasive operations that it is beyond the effective reach of the national policies of any country, free to some extent to make decisions in the interest of corporate efficiency alone." "Insisting," "primacy," "genuine," "sensitive," "respecting," "pervasive," "beyond the reach," and "corporate efficiency alone" are all somewhat colored words or phrases in which the multinational corporation comes off a good deal better than the other two.

For a different classification which regards corporations with more than 50 percent of sales as multinational, those with 25 to 50 percent as internationally oriented, and those with 10 to 24 percent as having significant foreign operations, see N. K. Bruck and F. A. Lees, "Foreign Content of U.S. Corporate Activities," *Financial Analysts Journal* (September–October 1966), pp. 1–6 (of reprint).

The national firm with foreign operations knows where it belongs. First and foremost it is a citizen of a particular country. Foreign operations are small in the total scheme of things. There may be an international division, rather than foreign operations in every division. The company is not speculating when it holds the currency of the nation claiming sovereignty over the parent corporation. Assuming it is an American corporation, its securities are issued in dollars, and its accounts kept in that currency. It may have substantial foreign ownership interests, but it feels at home only in one country, and substantially alien everywhere else.[2]

The multinational firm seeks to be a good citizen of each country where it has operations. It hires local executives, uses local directors to more than token extent, possibly admits local capital (but at what price?). Irritated by the United States government's Voluntary Credit Restraint Program of February 1965, the Canadian government issued "Guiding Principles for Good Corporate Behavior," which were summarized in the Task Force Report as follows:

> Firms are to strive for "maximum competitiveness" and "appropriate specialization" within the international firms. Market opportunities are to be exploited at home and abroad, natural resources processed in Canada where economic to do so, and Canadian procurement sources searched out and developed. A pricing policy fair to both the company and to Canadians is to be pursued, "including sales to the parent company and other affiliates." R and D capacity is to be developed. Sufficient earnings are to

2. See Stephen H. Hymer, "The International Operations of National Firms: A Study of Direct Investment."

be retained to support the growth of the Canadian operation. Firms are to work toward a Canadian outlook within management, and include "a major portion of Canadian citizens on its Board of Directors." Firms are "periodically to publish information on the financial position and operation of the company" and "to have the objective of a financial structure which provides opportunity for equity participation in the Canadian enterprise by the Canadian public." They are to recognize and share "national objectives" and "encourage and support Canadian institutions directed toward the intellectual, social and cultural advancement of the community."[3]

The issues are familiar to those who have borne with me through these lectures. It would be easy to ask ironic questions about possible conflicts between different requirements, such as "maximum competitiveness" and "fair pricing," or "economic behavior" and "following Canadian national objectives." But the thrust is clear. Efficiency and citizenship normally converge. When they occasionally diverge, the requirements of citizenship are to take precedence. In promulgating the "Guiding Principles," the Canadian government informed the subsidiaries of foreign corporations that there was already wide adherence to the principles, but that room remained for improvement. If it is granted that this is the case, the interesting question is whether improved Canadian citizenship would reduce profits of the corporation, or merely correct the distortion of efficient allocation which had

3. Task Force, *Foreign Ownership and the Structure of Canadian Industry*, pp. 231–32.

been imposed on the corporation by the home country.[4]

The international corporation has no country to which it owes more loyalty than any other, nor any country where it feels completely at home. It equalizes the return on its invested capital in every country, after adjustment for risk which is free of the myopia that says home investment is automatically risk-free and all foreign investments are risky. It is willing to speculate against the currency of the head office because it regards holdings of cash anywhere as subject to exchange risks which should be hedged.

There may well be criteria of business organization by which companies can be categorized as to whether they are national firms with foreign operations, multinational firms, or international corporations—criteria of which I am unaware. The criteria I would pose are two: the company's attitudes toward foreign-exchange risks and toward equalization of profits. The attitudes may be subconscious rather than articulated. The national corporation is usually hedged in foreign exchange, is seldom long of foreign currencies, and is ready to go short when a foreign currency is under attack. It will not take a short position in the currency of the parent company and does not, in fact, recognize that it has an exchange position when it holds net assets denominated in money in that currency. A multinational firm would regard it as a

4. I may refer again, perhaps, to my review of Safarian's *Foreign Ownership of Canadian Industry,* which suggested that the profits of U.S. corporations in Canada were already lower than one might anticipate—though the evidence is limited—because of the demands of Canadian citizenship, and Robin Mathews' letter to *The Canadian Forum,* cited in n. 23 of the second lecture, asserting that U.S. subsidiaries in Canada were "intimately linked with the self-regarding policies of national and nationalist governments," and specifically of the United States.

breach of good citizenship to go short of a foreign currency. The international firm, on the other hand, is conscious of the exchange risks it takes in any currency, including that of the parent country. Royal Dutch Shell cannot relax when it has net monetary assets in sterling, if sterling is weak, merely because its head office is incorporated as a British company. This would fail to maximize the total value of the company worldwide.

The test of returns on assets in different countries is impossible to apply, both because one lacks proxy variables for the subjective discounts for risk applied in various countries and because of ignorance of the time horizon over which profits are maximized. Notionally, however, the criterion is as follows: a national firm with foreign operations must earn a higher return on foreign than on home investment because the former is risky, the latter risk-free. A multinational firm starts out like a national firm with foreign operations, but after time each national operation takes on a life of its own, with its own rate of profit, which the parent company accepts and which is related to the future growth of the national subsidiary mainly as a source of finance. There is no thought of closing down or selling off a subsidiary because its long-run profit prospects are below what could be earned on the assets elsewhere. Good citizens do not emigrate. The international corporation, on the other hand, will equalize at the margin everywhere in the world, subject of course, to the discount for risk which applies realistically at home as well as abroad.

Implicit or explicit in the attitudes of many observers are criteria which relate these designations to the political goals of countries. The national corporation is presumably subservient to the national political purposes of its sovereign. The multinational corporation tries to thread its way among multiple claims on its loyalty, moving boldly when these converge and hedging when they conflict. The international corporation is committed to carry out the will of no country as it obeys the laws of all. This may be true in theory; the reality is otherwise. A country can exercise pressure on a corporation in proportion to the volume of assets in that country. In general, the country that can exert the greatest pressure on the company's policies will be the largest and richest country, or that where the company originated and where its management is resident. The risk of pressure is reduced by making the assets in any one jurisdiction depend for their efficient use on other assets outside the jurisdiction. This lowers the temptation for the country to take over the firm's investment. But while it is possible for the assets in a jurisdiction to be worth little to the sovereign power, they remain important to the investing corporation. To this extent it is impossible for the international corporation to escape all political pressure of national governments, or to move beyond their reach, as the Task Force definition asserts.

Whether today's direct investments constitute international corporations, multinational firms, or national firms with foreign operations is a factual question which the reader may decide for himself. But I should like to suggest the hypothesis that national firms with foreign operations are in process of evolving into multinational firms and showing signs of ultimate evolution to international corporations. This much is factual. I further suggest that the international corporation can develop as a monopolist or as an instrument of national goals, which conflict with world efficiency, or it can operate in the cosmopolitan interest to spread technology, reallocate capital, and enlarge competition. The choice is not solely up to the corporation. It depends largely on national policies toward the corporation. Policy may be laissez-faire (or almost laissez-faire; it is impossible to escape the residual intervention of a non-neutral tax system). Or it may be interventionist in one or more directions: to maximize national income, regardless of the effect on the rest of the world, or to join with other countries in harmonized policies in the general interest.

Dependent then on the nature of their behavior and the character of the environment within which they operate, as determined by governmental policies of an independent, contradictory, or harmonized type, international corporations can represent a boon, a bane, or a nullity. It is entirely possible, perhaps inescapable, that different observers with different evaluations of the behavior of the corporations and the character of their environment as shaped by government will arrive at very different conclusions as to which they are.

The Corporation as a Monopolist in a World of Laissez-Faire

The national corporation rose to prominence in the United States in about the 1890s and was regarded as a monopolist. Trusts, as they were called, used one or another sort of discriminatory device to force small competitors to the wall and, once they had eliminated competition, to raise prices again. Note that there had to be an asymmetry about exit and entry to permit prices to be raised to the same level as before the attack. Unless reentry was more difficult than exit, a monopolist could not raise the price back to the old level without reattracting the old competitors. The asymmetry may have been real economies of scale which enabled the aggressive price cutter to make enlarged profits at lower prices than he could before the small fry had been driven out. Prices then fell and reentry was impossible. Or the asymmetry might simply have been that the trust with its monopoly profits stood ready to cut prices again in the market of a reentering firm, and so discouraged reentry. In this latter case, but not the former, the trust brought about a real loss to the world owing to monopoly, with entry limited, and output lower and prices higher than they had been under competitive conditions. This was the basis for the antitrust movement in the United States that produced the Sherman Act of 1890 and the Clayton Act of 1914.

Pure monopolies are rare in world trade today. The deBeers diamond syndicate, which markets not only the diamonds of South Africa but also the gem diamonds of the Soviet Union, can be cited as one example. The International Nickel Corporation, which controls not only the world's largest nickel mines in Sudbury, Ontario, but has shown an interest in acquiring new properties as they are discovered in New Caledonia, Petsamo, Finland, or Cuba, is another. The oil industry of the 1920s qualified during the days of the "As Is" and "Red Line" agreements.

But monopolistic competition remains an issue: the purchase by Alcan of Aardal og Sunndal Verk in aluminum, that by Gillette of the Braun company making electric razors in Germany, the spillover of United States firms that cannot expand within the country into horizontal integration outside, or the steady expansion of vertical integration which makes new entry more and more difficult by enlarging the ante one needs to amass in order to join the game. This is an important score against takeovers as opposed to new investment, Hymer rightly emphasizes; takeovers leave the number of mar-

keting organizations in an industry unchanged or reduced, while new entry enlarges the number of competing units.

Monopoly, then, is one basis of direct investment and
of international growth of the national corporation.

The Corporation as a Perfector of Markets in a World of Laissez-Faire

But the extension of the national corporation into
international operations does not necessarily reduce competition. It may well increase it. Local monopoly, which
flourishes in markets cut off from world trade through
costs of overcoming distance, ignorance, inertia, or protectionist policies, may be undone by international investment, which overcomes distance and tariffs and at-
tacks ignorance and inertia. Just as the national corporation in the United States increased efficiency by breaking
up local monopolies in separate markets which ordinary
commerce did not eliminate, so the international corporation can increase rather than reduce competition.

A special case of market failure in innovation because
of the difficulty in distributing the risks of investment
needed at several stages of production has been discussed
in an earlier lecture. Here vertical integration improves
efficiency, rather than undermines it, by internalizing the
risks of innovation and enabling them to be met as one.

Larger corporations, vertically or horizontally integrated, may also reduce costs and increase efficiency in
world resource allocation as a result of long-run falling
cost curves and lower prices through historically down-
ward shifts of upward sloping supply curves, through
learning by doing, or by other scale economies, external
to the firm, which do not violate the competitive condi-

tions. To the extent that these sources of efficiency have not been exploited, the rise of the international corporation is likely to increase efficiency, as the rise of the national corporation is claimed to have done nationally.

There is more to it than merely lower costs. The national corporation in the United States has been an engine for increasing economic efficiency as it raises capital in the cheapest market and brings it to the cheapest sources of labor. By this means it tends to equalize both wages and the cost of capital throughout the country, and in a fashion which factor markets, apart from the labor market in two world wars, has been unable to do. Factor-price equalization in the United States has a long way still to go, though it has come a considerable distance. Trade among regions seems unable to achieve identical returns for labor and capital in all regions, as does factor movement. Prior to the rise of the national corporation, interest rates were high and wages low in the South and West compared with the East and Middle West. Since 1890 factor markets have been improved by the occasional strong demands associated with war and inflation. But the movement of national corporations to the South and West has certainly assisted in the process, lowering the price of capital and raising the return to labor, and operating alongside goods and factor markets to increase efficiency and welfare.

The national corporation with foreign operations and the multinational corporation cannot work with equal efficiency in the direction of factor-price equalization so long as they are handicapped by economic risks, exchange risks, risks of governmental intervention in trade, or even risks of confiscation. The multinational corporation, for example, borrows locally where it can, in preference to acquiring capital in the cheapest market, because it seeks to minimize exchange risks by matching localized assets with liabilities in the same locality. It hesitates to undertake production in one country for sale in another, despite cost advantages. Only a handful of United States corporations have undertaken production abroad for distribution in the United States or have rationalized very thoroughly their European production and distribution facilities to take advantage of least-cost locations. The point has long been made that the United States corporation in Europe is in a better position to take advantage of the European Economic Community than local firms, because they have no roots and can readily move from one country to another in search of cost advantages. This advantage is primarily potential rather than actual, however. New investors plan locations to accommodate themselves to relative costs, including tax concessions available from regional authorities in one country or another. Existing firms hesitate. "To sell in France, produce in France." It is still not certain that the E.E.C. is permanent and unchanging and that there may not reappear national policies in the fields of tariffs and quotas, exchange rates, excise taxes, freight rates, and so on.

In a world of laissez-faire, however, with no tariffs, with fixed exchange rates, and with, say, minimal taxation because of minimal government, the international corporation which scanned a world horizon would be more than likely to improve the efficiency of goods and factor markets that function less than optimally because of distance, ignorance, and local monopoly. The possible exceptions make it necessary to talk in terms of likelihoods rather than certainties: monopoly, declining costs of the infant-industry variety, and external diseconomies. Monopoly has been discussed. The infant-industry possibility might mean that some efficient locations of industry never got under way because of the dominance of an efficient international firm which failed to see the long-run, low-cost potential of an existing high-cost site.

External diseconomies produce overcrowding and social losses in excessive traffic, pollution and need for public capital in locations crowded into by private investment at a time when locations with excess social capacity are being ignored. The point can perhaps be put most sharply by quoting the title of the book by J.-F. Gravier, *Paris et le désert français.*[5] National French corporations have turned their backs on their regional origins to move to the capital. In the European Common Market, the same phenomenon, which the Rome treaty sought to counter by establishing the European Investment Bank and the European Social Fund, is found in the magnetic pull of private enterprise to the central core of the market and away from peripheral southern Italy, southwest France, Brittany, and eastern Bavaria to the Paris-Brussels-Amsterdam-Cologne center. Something of the same hydrocephalic tendency may be observed in New York, London, and the Milan-Turin-Genoa Golden Triangle. But much of the agglomerative pull represents real economies of proximity, by no means entirely offset by external social diseconomies: the coalescence of market areas is economical for the shopper; face-to-face contacts for non-routine managerial operations like finance, advertising, and legal consultation make decision-making surer and more efficient. This last, indeed, is the advantage that national firms have over those whose decision center is abroad.

By and large, just as the national firm on balance in-

5. 2d ed. Paris, Flammarion, 1958.

creased the efficiency of goods and factor markets within a country, so the international corporation has the capacity for increasing the efficiency of international goods and factor markets. The conditions required for factor-price equalization through trade exist neither within a large country like the United States nor worldwide. Equalization through factor movements is undesirable for migration, so long as the country of emigration has not accomplished its Malthusian revolution and begun family limitation. If emigrants are replaced by additions to population in countries that are at the Malthusian subsistence level, the only impact of migration is to reduce levels of living in the country of immigration.[6] Capital markets seem to function better among countries and regions of the same level of development than they do in moving capital from rich areas to poor. Supported by interregional trade and factor movements, the national corporation has gone some distance (but not all the way) in equalizing wages and interest rates between North

6. For two views of the migration of skilled personnel to developed countries—the "cosmopolitan," or "international," which emphasizes the increase in world output from employing people where they can earn the highest return, and the "national," which regards emigration of skilled people as having strong external diseconomies for the country of emigration—see Walter Adams, ed., *The Brain Drain* (New York, Macmillan, 1968), and especially the essays by Harry G. Johnson and Don Patinkin, representing the cosmopolitan and national schools, respectively. The distinction between the two models runs closely parallel to the distinction implied for direct investment. The cosmopolitan school would argue that the international firm increases allocative efficiency, or will do so when it moves out of the multinational to the international stage; the national school puts weight on the infant-industry argument, on external diseconomies, or on the purely political value of the preservation of national independence as contrasted with integration into larger units or the world.

and South and East and West in the United States. The
international corporation can supplement trade and factor movements in moving toward equalization of incomes
among developed countries, say, North America, Europe,
the Dominions, and Japan. It offers a possibility of greater equalization between rich and poor countries, where
factor movements and trade have done and seem to be
able to do very little to produce equalization.

The International Corporation in a World of
Governments with Positive Purposes

It adds great complication to move from laissez-faire
to a world with discrete national governments, each
equipped with a social welfare function it is trying to
maximize. Three cases may be distinguished: one in
which government seeks to use the international corporation, or more exactly the national corporation with
foreign operations, to accomplish its national purposes;
one where the corporation maximizes its profits in the
short run by taking advantage of divergences among national policies, and particularly among national tax laws;
and one where the corporation tries to live as a good
citizen of each country in which it operates, even at the
cost of not maximizing profits in the short run, believing
that this is the way to maximize profits or the life of the
corporation over some indefinite time span running long
into the future.

In a Marxian analysis, national business and government are difficult or impossible to disentangle. A national corporation operating abroad is thus an instrument of foreign policy, or diplomatic representatives in
a foreign land are tools of business imperialism, which-
ever interpretation comes most readily to hand. Interna-

tional business is neocolonialism, and foreign policy is capitalistic exploitation, with little purpose served by trying to make nice distinctions. There are times and occasions when the point of view seems apposite, as, for example, in the close relations between the Ministry of Fuel and Power in the United Kingdom and the two major British international oil companies, or in the sureness with which the Department of State in the United States asserts that subsidiaries of United States companies in foreign countries must under no circumstances trade with Cuba or China.

But Marxian analysis is surely too sweeping. Government and business interests may converge from time to time, and when they diverge one or the other may yield. They frequently collide head-on. Business has its private purpose of making profits within some spatial horizon and over some time horizon which its management chooses. Government has its public purposes of varied sorts: to collect revenue, protect consumers against monopoly, carry out foreign policy, manage the balance of payments—purposes which are legitimate in the public interest and which may well run counter to the profitability of the international company. In domestic affairs, the government lays down the law to the corporation. In the international sphere, the matter is more complex. Government may try to direct business in what to do, but there are other governments, with their own purposes, with interests at issue. If the two governments fail to coordinate or harmonize their action, the company may slide between their separate jurisdictions, or suffer from being clobbered twice.

Hymer has expressed the view that the relationship of governments to the international corporation is asymmetrical. The home-country government will instruct the

parent corporation as to how to make the subsidiary behave abroad, while the host-country government is unlikely to undertake to lay out policy for the parent company in the home country through the intermediary of
the subsidiary. This is probably the case, but it may have
more to do with the particular view of international law
taken by the United States than with the inherent power
position. Surely the United States has never hesitated to
raise questions with home-country governments through
subsidiaries of foreign corporations in the United States.
The sale of American Viscose by Courtaulds during the
war, the suit to prove that General Aniline and Film was
German-owned, not Swiss, are cases that leap to mind on
this side of the water; and the French government did
not shilly-shally in putting pressure on Caltex to sell off
part of its investment in refineries and distribution facilities in France to the French chosen instrument in the
petroleum field. The interests of the host country may
well diverge from that of the company and of the home
government in matters of antitrust, balance of payments,
tax revenue, and even foreign policy, and the host is not
without leverage. Foreign-exchange control, price control, access to capital markets, ordinary and extraordinary
taxation, licensing, inspections, a variety of weapons
short of confiscation are at hand, and in the final analysis
the power of eminent domain. Host country like home
country can exert pressure on the corporation.

This pressure may be of two sorts: to prevent the corporation from acting against the cosmopolitan and incidentally the national interest; or, when the corporation wants to act in the most efficient way from a world
point of view, to interfere with that. Tax systems inevitably distort allocation, if only the allocation of effort.
Two tax systems in two countries, constructed indepen-

dently, are virtually certain to create opportunities for an international corporation to maximize net profits after tax in a way that departs from the optimal allocation of production and distribution on a before-tax basis. But even apart from taxes, government may insist on exports from high-cost producers because it is maintaining an overvalued exchange rate and is unable to construct a system of subsidies that would produce the pattern of exports at an equilibrium rate. Government consistently attracts foreign investment by efficiency-distorting tariffs. It may be greedy for taxes, seek to convert foreign investors in its natural resources into a monopoly or cartel, or take over an existing monopoly or cartel in order to siphon off profits as taxes. Government may be neutral with respect to efficiency, and corporations distort. Corporations may be efficient, and governments distort. Or one may distort in one way and the other may compound the difficulty, or merely accept it.

It must not be thought for a minute that all governmental intervention in international business is merely distortionary. Government has its legitimate interests, and the existence of the international corporation limits its effectiveness in pursuing them. Some of these limitations may be exaggerated, as we have suggested in previous lectures, such as the inability of the French government to plan if international corporations have investments in France, or of Canada to operate monetary policy if one small bank is owned abroad. There is nonetheless something to the case that the existence of instrumentalities that are partly within the jurisdiction and partly outside limits the capacity of government to carry out its functions. If the United States government decides, rightly or wrongly, that American citizens should not sell to Cuba, dummy corporations in Canada which bought from United States corporations and passed the goods along to Cuba could defeat this policy. The French policy on direct investment at one stage in its evolution was defeated by the welcome reception given to United States investment by Belgium and Italy. The existence of several jurisdictions side by side means that the government of one is limited in its effectiveness. State and local governments understand this in the United States. High taxes on cigarettes, liquor, personal income, corporate income, and so forth, lead to purchases outside the state or to migration. Governments no less than corporations must compete to attract business when it has mobility which extends beyond the confines of a single country.

This leads us to the second model of the international corporation which maximizes income between the interstices of the overlapping and underlapping laws laid down by government. James E. Meade suggests in *Trade and Welfare*[7] that if two countries have different tax systems, country A taxing production and country B taxing consumption, people will work in B and live in A, with wasteful commuting, loss of government revenue, and failure to meet goals. It is worse than that. Just as some states with no notable economic advantages cut prices on incorporation or corporate taxes to attract companies to make their headquarters there, so countries will compete for the international corporation. Luxembourg, Liechtenstein, the Bahamas, and a number of Swiss cantons are rivals for the position among countries that Delaware has among states. The competition is hotting up. The tax concessions given to the national corporation by Mississippi, Arkansas, Georgia, and others in the United States have their counterpart both in tax

7. London, Oxford University Press, 1955.

concessions, as illustrated in the last lecture for the less developed countries, and in regional subsidies in Europe United States unwillingness to conclude tax-sparing agreements with other countries may be an important factor in preventing this governmental price-cutting from going further.

The evolution has thus far stopped short of the international corporation at the stages of the national corporation with foreign operations or the multinational corporation and this prevents the problem of international corporations trading one government off against another from going very far. The fact that one country will tax the income of a corporation on its foreign earnings, to the extent that they are not already taxed abroad, underlines the point. Foreign earnings are brought back to the home country rather than distributed directly to stockholders from a corporate head-office in some low-tax jurisdiction, and home-country governments can decide what earnings under what circumstances qualify for the tax credit. In other problems such as balances of payments or antitrust, the power of the home country and of the host remains important so long as corporations are unwilling to shift jurisdiction to evade it. But divergences among national policies give the corporation at each stage of its evolution considerable room for maneuver even if it cannot achieve the lowest common denominator of control in each area.

Take antitrust policy. The United States has strong antitrust traditions. Other countries do not. The United States asserts that it opposes any restraint of trade which affects the United States market. It is evidently powerless to prevent the deBeers diamond syndicate from organizing the market for gem diamonds, and keeping prices up for fiancés in the United States. It asserts that it can control the activities of United States corporations that engage in agreements abroad to restrict sales to the United States. But can it? If United States corporations license their technology to foreigners, there is likely to be an implicit if not explicit understanding about sales in the home market of the licensor; where such corporations construct or acquire foreign subsidiaries, they clearly control marketing from abroad by those subsidiaries; and where foreign subsidiaries of United States companies are permitted under the laws of foreign countries or, not permitted, are inadequately policed, they may well alter the desire of foreign firms to sell in the United States market. It may well be that effective antitrust surveillance is a will-o'-the-wisp at best, as many sophisticated or cynical observers think. But the maintenance of import competition with domestic production is very much reduced when United States corporations go abroad to consort with foreign firms in jurisdictions that have little interest or tradition in antitrust matters.

Our third possibility in a world of governments with positive purposes, after corporations that serve the purpose of one country and corporations that slide between the cracks of underlapping national jurisdictions, is the multinational corporation which tries to be a good citizen everywhere. This, of course, is what all corporations claim to do. It is difficult to accept the claim at its face value. Corporations want profits. They also want peace and quiet. As much as possible they want to become like citizens of the host country, invisible to the public eye, fading into the background, so long as it gives them peace and quiet at not too large a price in profits. But some aspects of citizenship spell trouble. The multinational corporation is usually 100 percent foreign-owned because large minority interests breed conflicts of interest which mean trouble. They prefer not to publish their accounts, if the advantage they bring to direct investment is substantial and their profits large, because this means notoriety. A certain amount, even 100 percent, of management and direction from the host country is tolerable so long as it does not run profits down too much. In the best of all possible worlds, it is more, not less, profitable to have local management. The early mistakes of the large multinational corporation which closed down unprofitable operations of Frigidaire at Gennevilliers or Remington Rand near Lyon are not likely to be repeated. Tradition is treated circumspectly. With time, the United States corporation may well become like the British firms in New Zealand and Australia, indistinguishable in most respects from native industry.

This model applies to inframarginal direct investment. Old firms will grow perhaps at a somewhat faster pace than local industry because of the advantages of better access to technology and capital than local firms, but they will not get far out of line. If the country grows slowly, direct investment will also grow slowly, despite the fact that the firm would make higher profits by transferring its assets to a faster-growing environment. New investment at the margin will be guided by profit prospects; old will proceed at the pace, or a little better, of domestic companies.

There is a valid basis for this attitude in the insurance principle of spreading risks. Back in the fifties before convertibility, I asked a comptroller of a large international corporation how foreign-exchange controls affected the company's investment decisions. He replied that it did not affect them: "We have assets in seventy countries all over the world. Some substantial portion of them at any one time will block the transfer of profits.

But this will never be true of them all. If we can make profits in local currency, we can transfer enough home from some countries to make it worthwhile." By the same token, too close a watch on the level of profits in foreign investment in all countries to equalize returns at the margin may be dysfunctional. The rate of growth in various countries and parts of the world will wax and wane, in this view, but it pays to stay with investments during the waning periods for the subsequent waxing.

I must confess that I am somewhat sceptical of this proposition as it applies to Europe. Many of the firms that went to Europe in the 1960s were impressed by the very rapid rate of growth in the 1950s through about 1963 and anticipated that this represented a long-run trend. I do not think so. Elsewhere I have explained why this "supergrowth" was due not to superior macroeconomic policies, planning, incomes policy, or the like, but to a combination of a once-and-for-all technological leap after the war in a wide number of fields, plus an elastic labor supply which held down wages, reallocated labor from low-efficiency to highly productive jobs, and maintained high levels of capital formation. When the infinite labor supply was exhausted, growth declined to more normal rates.[8]

The multinational firm, however, may not be permitted to go native in this fashion. It still must face the positive purposes of two or more governments, that of the parent company and those of its subsidiaries. These policies may run parallel or fail to overlap. In this happy

8. See my *Europe's Postwar Growth: The Role of the Labor Supply* (Cambridge, Mass., Harvard University Press, 1967); and Edward F. Denison, *Why Growth Rates Differ* (Washington, D.C., The Brookings Institution, 1967).

event, the multinational corporation responds fully to multinational directives. They may conflict. In this case the firm must struggle along as best it can. Difficulty presses in the balance-of-payments sphere. The host country says, "Bring home profits"; the host country says, "Reinvest profits." The home country says, "Invest abroad if you like, but don't export capital"; the host country says, "Invest in this country, if you must, but bring money."[9]

Life, of course, is full of such impossible situations where two authorities, each with some control over an individual or institution, push in opposite or diverging directions. As children we learn to cope with two parental authorities. The corporation may succeed in sliding between the jurisdictions; it may get hung up subject to both of them, as for example in double taxation, or— most probable—it will muddle along.

Harmonizing Policies with Respect to the International Corporation

If the most effective use of the international corporation is to be made, however, so that it will neither distort efficient economic allocation by sliding between underlapping independent tax and rule-making jurisdictions nor find itself pinned down by overlapping sovereigns, it is necessary to harmonize national policies toward the international corporation. The effort has a further purpose: to prevent the home country from using the cor-

9. Australia publicized a desire for foreign investors to convert foreign exchange into Australian pounds, rather than relying on investment in kind, i.e. patents, technology, equipment, and borrowing the rest locally. It is said that Britain today seeks to require foreign companies to bring from abroad 100 percent of the fixed capital of an investment, but is prepared to bargain case by case.

poration as a means of achieving its foreign-policy purposes outside of normal diplomatic channels. The task is difficult; some would wish it impossible.

Harmonization of economic policies is a concept that emerged from customs union, and in particular from the European Economic Community. It was quickly found that it was insufficient to remove tariffs to achieve free movement of goods, services, and factors in customs union in a nondistortionary fashion. One could not even remove the customs officials from the frontier until excise tax rates had been harmonized. Other forms of discrimination remained and had to be winkled out, one by one: the harmonization of transport rates, so that railroad freight journeys across the border were priced the same per mile as internal tariffs rather than as two short and high-priced trips; turnover taxes, organized on the basis of value-added or cascaded, and on consumption or production, which unless harmonized could give double taxation for trade in some direction and none in the other; social security taxation, at least in the eyes of some observers; systems of subsidizing agriculture; and so on. Many economists think that economic integration implies a fixed set of exchange rates, in turn implying harmonized monetary and fiscal policies. And if harmonized taxation, then harmonized benefits, lest industry in one country, for example, have to pay for services provided free by the state in another. And antitrust policy. And so on again.

In the European Economic Community, it may be necessary to go further and establish a common law for corporations, including provision for European incorporation which would entitle companies to equal rights (and duties) in all states. The measures are difficult and take time.

In international intercourse, countries enter into agreements, giving up freedom of action on their own part in order to obtain desired treatment by others. Lacking agreements with each country seeking to maximize its own income or wealth, one is apt to get optimum tariffs to raise export and reduce import prices, and retaliation. Agreement eliminates beggar-thy-neighbor behavior at home and abroad. It abrogates sovereignty to a degree, as all international agreement does, indeed as all international intercourse does. The world since 1944 has laid down rules for the application of tariffs in trade, the operation of exchange rates, the need for nations to account to the world for their domestic monetary and fiscal policies. It is not without interest that import restrictions have not been applied in the monetary troubles of 1967 and 1968, save for the temporary surcharges by Britain in 1966, because of the General Agreement on Tariffs and Trade (GATT).

The draft charter of the International Trade Organization, which was the moribund intellectual antecedent of GATT, included provision for international rules and regulations governing monopoly. They did not survive the sea change from the I.T.O., which could not be negotiated as a treaty, to GATT, which was adopted as an intergovernmental agreement with no need for legislative ratification. The United Nations made a passing attempt to study international cartels with a view to adopting international standards. GATT has been urged from time to time to look into one aspect of monopolistic competition, i.e. dumping, or international price discrimination, but this also gets nowhere. The field is a difficult one at best.

Business interests from time to time devise international codes of national behavior toward foreign invest-

ment. Understandably, these mainly focus on the rights
of corporations and the duties of governments toward
their guests, with emphasis on their immunity to confiscation, or on the need in extreme circumstances for
adequate, prompt, and effective compensation with arbi-
tration of disputes in an environment friendly to business, as, for example, Switzerland.

Economists concerned with the growth of less developed countries, on the other hand, have from time to
time turned their hands to drafting commitments which
the less developed countries might impose on each other
and foreign business. These would both put a halt to
competitive seduction of direct investment by eager can-
didates for development and require such firms as did
invest to commit themselves to expensive programs of
training, indigenization, reinvestment, restricted remittance of profits, and so forth. As the last lecture suggested,
both these partisan initiatives are likely to be unavail-
ing, given the wide spread in the bargaining positions
of individual countries and companies on each side of
the fence. Countries that can easily attract investment
will want a stern code for companies; not so the countries that get few nibbles. Conversely, companies that
have advantages of technology, capital, management,
and markets in scarce supply in certain industries will
want standards too rich for the blood of the marginal
direct investors. Failure to make progress along these
lines was easily predicted.

One possible line of action would be for the United
States and perhaps a few of the leading European direct
investors to adopt a series of self-denying ordinances
under which they would give up the aggressive protection of the interests of their foreign investors on the one
hand, and the attempt to carry out domestic policy

through such investments on the other. This would leave the major foreign investors at the tender mercies of the host governments. The farsighted among the latter would know that it paid to deal "fairly" with direct investors; the myopic would quickly learn. The precedent for unilateral concessions of this sort is ample. Big boys fight with one hand tied behind their backs. The developed countries extended concessions on tariff items under the Kennedy Round to the less developed countries without asking for reciprocal concessions, though it is necessary to mention that most of the items of interest to the less developed countries were excluded from the negotiation from the beginning.

One need not feel moved by the plight of the investing corporations, if this were done. Many of them are as big as or bigger than the countries with which they deal in sales, assets, and skill of management, if not in sovereign powers. Less readily acceptable is the cession of sovereignty to the corporations themselves, who would be freed of the surveillance of government of the developed countries in important matters of the maintenance of competition and equitable payment of taxes, and, perhaps one should add although I do so with reluctance, impact on the balance of payments. No, the corporations are too large and powerful to turn them loose in a partial laissez-faire for the less developed countries to exploit to the extent of their appetite and capacity. Harmonization of rules for the international corporation is necessary if the institution is going to be effective in promoting world welfare. Such harmonization is difficult because of different national traditions, institutions, interests, pressures. It is nonetheless inescapable.

The Task Force in Canada at a number of places notes the need for international policies governing multina-

tional or international corporations, mentioning specifically the need to resolve the question of conducting
domestic policy through subsidiaries of domestic companies in a sort of extraterritoriality (p. 322), the harmonization of policies to maintain competition (p. 332),
cooperation in investment guarantees and even international charters (p. 396). It suggested in a fainthearted
way (p. 342) that Canada should take the lead in calling
for the conferences necessary to produce agreement on
these points, to which should be added the regulation
of transfer prices, and the division of tax revenues between countries. Reluctance to push harder seems to be
based on the view that the Canadian civil service would
like nothing better than to stall on the disagreeable task
of imposing Canadian regulation on foreign investment
in Canada, while pushing for international agreement
on which "no immediate results seem likely."

The French urged a host-country agreement on the
European Economic Community. The initiative lan-
guished because of the divergent interests of France and
Belgium and Italy.

Who should then bell the cat? In my judgment the
cat itself. It is the United States which is bitterly criticized. I should like to see this country call a conference
on the international corporation under the auspices of
the United Nations, rather along the lines of the United
Nations Conference on Trade and Development (although I recognize that that paradigm will send cold
shivers up and down the backs of the economic staffs of
many a foreign office). There should be a preparatory
commission, which should be given a couple of years to
prepare position papers and background material on
functional problems, and especially questions of competition, taxation, extraterritoriality, balances of payments,

including limitations on the right to export and discrimination in favor of imports from the parent, the conditions under which countries could discriminate against foreign as opposed to national investment, and possibly such questions as international charters for corporations. I should like to see emerge from that conference an international agency which would collect information on direct investment on a systematic basis, overall and case by case, and would have power to prohibit an investment that substantially reduced competition in a given commodity, even if both governments consented, as Canada and Norway have done in the Alcan-Aardal og Sunndal Verk takeover. There should be an international Ombudsman, staffed by experts from the smaller countries, to which companies could appeal if they were being unduly squeezed by overlapping sovereignty of two countries. Or governments that clashed head-on in their directions to a given firm and its subsidiary for balance-of-payments or political reasons could appeal to such an institution for the resolution of the conflict on the basis of general principle; it would be desirable if they bound themselves in advance to adhere to its decision.

The International Corporation and the Nation-State

The nation-state is just about through as an economic unit. General De Gaulle is unaware of it as yet, and so are the Congress of the United States and right-wing know-nothings in all countries. Tariff policy is virtually useless, despite the last-gasp struggles of the protectionists to keep out Japanese steel, Danish cheese, Middle East oil, Brazilian powdered coffee, and of the Johnson administration to get the American public to stop going

abroad. Monetary policy is in the process of being inter-
nationalized. The world is too small. It is too easy to get
about. Two-hundred-thousand-ton tank and ore carriers
and containerization (to use an ugly hybrid), airbuses,
and the like will not permit sovereign independence of
the nation-state in economic affairs.

This is not to say that everything has to be decided
at the top. The soundest principle in administration is
that decision should be relegated to the lowest and small-
est possible level. The international corporation will
decentralize for all but a few crucial decisions, but it is
these that are vital to its economizing function. Similarly
the nation-state, along with the state, the city, the town,
but not perhaps the county, will survive and flourish.

Will the corporation really go international? The faint
beginnings appear. A Canadian is president of the Standard Oil Company of New Jersey and a Venezuelan sits
on the Board of Directors. A Frenchman has just become
president of the I.B.M. World Trade Corporation. It
is dangerous to extrapolate from only two points (though
economists do it). Ease of communication brings not only
officers from the parent to the field, but the personnel
and the point of view of the field to the head office. As
part of that process it may with time become more and
more difficult to distinguish head from foot or brain
from hands. The national firm with foreign operations
easily evolves into the multinational corporation.
Whether it continues on and becomes an international
corporation may turn on whether the nationals of the
host countries working for subsidiaries become more and
more internationally mobile.

In the United States, the corporation executive has
local roots in few cases. Left long in one locality, he may
develop them, as his children get toward high school.

In the move of Lever Brothers from Cambridge to New York, many an executive chose to remain behind. It is the boast of Atlanta, Georgia, that the same victory of local roots over corporate duty is time and again won in that city. But in the main, the American belongs to the company, or to a company since he is ready to change allegiances, rather than to a community. The company may move to Florida better to recruit engineers who like swimming, or to southern California for amenities which sunshine affords there. But a man recruited out of the Harvard Business School or the Wharton School is ready for any assignment. Ten years ago it was any assignment in the United States. Today it is any assignment at home or abroad. When Sloan Fellows at M.I.T. began to get restless in March and April, like horses headed for the barn, they ask each other, "Where are you likely to go?" It is rare that a young executive of a major company will be sent back to his old assignment, certainly not functionally, and probably not geographically. American executives of United States corporations are mobile among foreign subsidiaries. Foreign nationals working for United States-owned corporations are likely to be transferable at first only between their own country and the head office, although a company like General Motors may staff its Australian operations with a top executive from Vauxhall in Britain.[10]

In the long run it seems likely that the international corporation will develop a cadre of international executives, parallel, it may be noted, to the international civil servants of the United Nations, the European Economic Community, the Organization for Economic Coopera-

10. See Harnett, *Big Wheels and Little Wheels*. Note that Mr. Harnett settled permanently in Australia, rather than move on within the company, much as its boosters claim happens in Atlanta.

tion and Development, and the North Atlantic Treaty Organization of a few years back, who are mobile. The French contingents may not be truly international but available only for detached duty between home and particular assignments abroad. (Such is true of French international civil servants, and it reflects a particular attachment to the homeland which is muted in other countries.) This staff of executives is likely to be committed to the aggrandizement of the corporation, and of their own incomes and stock options, which will overwhelm any tendency in the multinational corporation for separate subsidiaries to behave like national corporations. The Canadian "presence" in the management of subsidiaries of foreign corporations in Canada, whether through management or directors, is not likely in the long run to prevail in favor of Canadian national objectives over the requirements of efficiency. If Canada wants such objectives, it must achieve them through positive direction of corporations by government. A superior course of action in my judgment, because internationalist rather than nationalist, is the development of harmonized international policies to regulate the international corporation.

At the moment, I think the multinational corporation is evolving into the international one faster than national governments are girding themselves to produce adequate policies to meet it. I suggest the need to hurry.

Index